girl be
BRAVE

girl be BRAVE

100 DAYS
TO CHART YOUR COURSE

CHERYL HALE

Abingdon Press
Growing in Life, Serving in Faith

GIRL BE BRAVE

100 DAYS TO CHART YOUR COURSE

Copyright © 2019 by Cherylann Hale Quinnelly

All rights reserved.

Library of Congress Cataloging-in-Publication data has been requested.

ISBN 978-1-5018-8540-2

Cover and interior design by Dexterity.

19 20 21 22 23 24 25 26—10 9 8 7 6 5 4 3 2 1
MANUFACTURED IN THE PEOPLE'S REPUBLIC OF CHINA

THIS BOOK IS

dedicated

TO ALL OF THOSE WHO ARE ASPIRING

to be brave.

Introduction

GIRL BE BRAVE.

I find these words powerful, and not just because my grandmother wrote them to my mother. They are special because I've never heard truer words in my life.

My grandmother, Frances, had a difficult life. She grew up in the rural South during the Great Depression. Her mother died when she was a toddler.

Her father, unable to raise her alone, sent her to live with her grandmother. Frances dropped out of school at a young age and married young, just like so many women in her generation.

She adored her husband, Ed, and for a while, their life was going well. They had five children, four rowdy boys and my mom, the tagalong.

Ed left Frances in the 1950s. This was a time when

women had few rights and no social structure existed to support single mothers. The older children, now grown, moved out to begin lives of their own. This left Frances and my mother to do their best to meet their basic needs. They struggled.

I was very close to Frances growing up, and my memories of her are vivid. I remember, when I was about eight years old, I was laying at the foot of her bed while she rocked in her chair in front of an open window. There was a gentle breeze and the faint sound of the gospel song "I'll Fly Away" playing in the background. Frances was reading her Bible with a magnifying glass. The image of her sitting there is burned into my memory. She was a woman of faith and perseverance. I'd like to think I have a little bit of her in me. Looking back at her old black-and-white photos, I can see the woman of defiant determination and courage that left such a huge mark on my life.

Fast forward to 2016. My mother was battling breast cancer. During the holidays, we had a family gathering, and I had the idea that we should read Frances' Bible.

In the back pages of my grandmother's Bible was a handwritten letter to her estranged husband and their children. In her southern, broken English, she pleaded with them to settle down and live decent lives. She wanted them to be the best version of themselves. The very last line of the heart-wrenching letter was to my mom, "girl be brave."

It struck me like lightning, and I knew in that moment what I had to do. Other people needed to hear these exact words. I wanted to shout them from the mountaintops, and I still do. That's why I founded the Girl Be Brave movement. I wanted Frances' words to vibrate through generations. We are able to maximize her impact by donating a portion of the proceeds of Girl Be Brave items to charity. It's a part of my vision to establish a Frances Hamilton scholarship fund for girls who don't have financial means.

Frances wrote that message to my mother because she knew my mother would need to be brave, and she was. My mother fought the fight of breast cancer and won. That's brave.

Life isn't easy; we all go through times of darkness and uncertainty. In those challenging periods, we all need to remind ourselves to be brave and to keep living, keep moving, until we find the light. We must overcome. We must be brave.

I've included some black-and-white photos of everyday women of today and long ago-women who, like Frances, radiate determination, courage, faith, and perseverance. May the words and photos inspire you to believe that you are brave. My grandmother would like that and so would I.

100 DAYS
TO CHART YOUR COURSE

ASK YOURSELF

WILL ACTING ON THESE EMOTIONS TAKE
YOU CLOSER OR FURTHER AWAY FROM
THE PERSON YOU WANT TO BE?

Day 1

THE POWER OF
OWNING YOUR EMOTIONS

One of the most powerful forces in your life are your emotions. On any given day, they can make or break you, assist you in **building** your life, or help you tear it down.

Your **emotions** are important. They need to be expressed, but you shouldn't live your life controlled by every emotion that passes through you. Emotions can take you to the highest of highs, but they can also push you to make a hasty choice that creates more harm than good. Some feelings just need to be **observed** and released.

When making decisions, it's important not to act on feeling alone. Feelings are fleeting. Use your **goals** to help you decide what action to take. Ask yourself if acting on these emotions will take you closer or further away from the person you want to be.

Nobody wants to live in emotional turmoil. In order to live a life of **peace** and sound decision-making, we need to learn to own our feelings and not let them own us.

Change Lanes

day 2

SOMETIMES YOU NEED TO CHANGE LANES

I don't know about you, but I like plans. I *really* like plans. I like goals and being productive. I like to know where I'm going and how long it will take to get there. The bliss of a carefully thought-out plan is something insanely *satisfying* to me.

One pitfall for being wired this way is that, at times, I love my plan more than I love the goal. That's a problem because sometimes along the way to your goal, you'll need to change lanes.

As we are traveling toward our glorious destination, the route we take to get there may turn out to be different than we expected. That's okay. Life is full of twists and turns that take us *exactly* where we need to be, when we need to get there.

I've learned to try not to cling too tightly to the plan but to still hang on to the goal. Clinging to the plan as though it's the only lifeline to achieving the goal can have dire consequences. We can get so caught up in working the plan that we fail to see the need for change or we don't consider that an unexpected opportunity could be instrumental in reaching the *destination*.

At the root of this planning desire is my need to feel in control, and more specifically, the need to control the unknown.

Sooner or later, we all realize we can't control everything or everyone. Loosening the reins a bit will allow space in the plan for unexpected divinity.

Make a plan, but let the road take you where it leads.

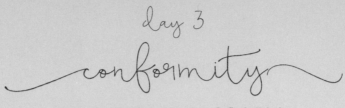

day 3

conformity

IS NOT NECESSARY

We live in a world that constantly pressures us into conforming to someone else's idea of who we're supposed to be. It's chronic fatigue for the *identity.*

Everywhere you turn, you'll find messages trying to convince you that your version of you just isn't right. Too skinny, too fat, too loud, too shy. . . .

The culprit isn't just pop culture and the degradation of society as a whole, it's something *much closer.*

Sometimes the pressure comes from a working mom reassuring herself and the decisions she's made by judging the stay-at-home mom or the stay-at-home mom belittling the working mother's choices. As women, we can be each other's worst enemy.

It doesn't have to be this way. People should *cheer* each other on, not participate in the world's mass push to turn us into online avatars. You haven't come this far in life by being somebody else. All your achievements, happy moments, and loving relationships are a byproduct of who YOU are. If you were to succumb to the pressure to conform, you would miss out on the *awesome* identity God has given you. He made you the you that you are because he knew what it would take to get you there. If he wanted you to be like Sally, he would have made you like her with all her desires and talents.

But in his infinite wisdom he knew the world would need someone like you with all of your *unique ideas* and abilities.

BE PREPARED
FOR A LITTLE RESISTANCE
ALONG THE WAY

I've never met anyone who accomplished anything worthwhile who didn't encounter some **resistance** along the way. It's inevitable.

Any noteworthy endeavor you set out to achieve is going to hit a few bumps. Nothing seems to go completely as planned, and you'll find yourself dealing with problems you didn't know you had.

That's okay. Don't be derailed by it. It's part of the **process.**

The old saying is true: It may not be easy, but it will be worth it.

If accomplishing big things were easy, everyone would do it. It seems as though we've become convinced the easy path is the right path.

Nothing could be further from the truth.

Not everything you are called to do will be easy. In fact, taking the right path is often **harder**. But don't worry, you can do hard things. It's a lie to believe you can't.

For me, being a wife and mother are a huge part of my purpose, but it certainly has not been the easiest task. With all the uncertainty of raising my children and building my marriage, it is by doing these acts that I have **grown** the most. Yes, some days (and years!) were hard, and at times, I felt like I wasn't enough, but I grew in those days. I became stronger and more **confident**. I learned more about myself through those holy callings.

That's a mighty task, but you're **capable**.

IF
ACCOMPLISHING
BIG THINGS
WERE EASY,
EVERYONE WOULD
DO IT.

DON'T **DIMINISH** YOURSELF TO EASE THE **INSECURITY** OF OTHERS.

DON'T WASTE
ANOTHER
PRECIOUS
MINUTE OF YOUR
LIFE REJECTING
YOURSELF.

day 6

SHE WANTS TO BE YOUR FRIEND

You know who. That girl in the mirror. The one in the reflection staring back at you. She really wants to be your friend. *Will you accept her?*

You will have many relationships throughout this life: friends, family, coworkers. But the person you have the closest, most intimate relationship with is yourself.

If you are like me, then you've wrestled with the image of the girl in the mirror. Judging her, rejecting her for all different reasons. Her nose is too big, her hair is too frizzy, and this and that and so on.

If you can get past what you think she should be and see her for who she really is, you will be able to really appreciate all she has to offer. Her kindness, her sense of humor, her loyalty to her family and friends, those things say so much more about a person than the size of her nose or hips.

She wants to be your friend, and she's crying out for you to embrace her. Accept her. *Make peace with her.*

Don't waste another precious minute rejecting yourself.

OPPORTUNITIES
COME TO PEOPLE
WHO ARE ALREADY
WALKING TOWARD
THEIR GOALS.

day 7

TAKE ACTION
EVEN IF IT'S SMALL

Actions are what separate those who live a life of purpose from those who sit it out, wondering why they never found fulfillment. So many wonderful people with **amazing gifts and ideas** never act on them. Those gifts go unexpressed.

There is no **"someday"** when it comes to action. Why not now? Why not start today? You don't have to wait until everything is perfect; it never will be. Do something now that will set you on your course. It doesn't matter how small the step is. A person can cover a lot of ground putting one foot in front of the other.

The first step can be the hardest. It's the **leaping off** from a place of security into the unknown that makes us hesitate, but you're stronger than you know. You can take this first step.

Momentum joins us when we take **action**. Opportunities begin to present themselves. I believe opportunities come to people who are already walking toward their goals. This momentum is a game changer because it multiplies your efforts. It's similar to a stone rolling downhill. Once it starts, it keeps going without relying on the efforts of the stone alone.

Think about the kind of world we would live in if everyone were acting on their God-given gifts and rising up to take action on the ideas they have in their hearts.

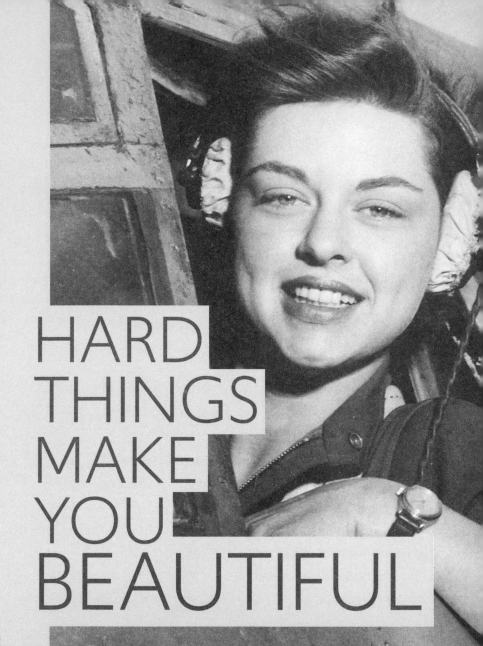

HARD
THINGS
MAKE
YOU
BEAUTIFUL

HARD THINGS MAKE YOU BEAUTIFUL

Yes, you heard that right. I believe it. When we go through difficult times, we grow. As we grow, we are humbled. The more humbled we are, the more human connections we create. The ability to connect with others on this level makes you beautiful because human connection is beautiful.

We learn from a young age to run away from hard stuff; we learn to avoid pain. But the problem with living to avoid pain is that it keeps you from living fully.

How many times have we avoided pain by binging on a half gallon of ice cream? Maybe instead of gorging ourselves on instant pleasures, we should press into the pain and be present in those difficult situations. We learn what we can and grow through it.

I've often found that on the other side of those hard times, I'm more aware and more empathetic. Others are going through the same types of pain. At least now I can see theirs because I also see mine. **I ALSO SEE ME.**

Resilience

Day 9

RESILIENCE

One major quality that I have found among those living their lives with purpose is *resilience*. Resilience is being able to get back up after being knocked down. Those with resilience can recover quickly. It's all in the rebound.

You don't have to be born with resilience; it's a *skill* you can develop.

I work toward being more resilient in my own life. I've found that after a major setback or failure, where I focus my thoughts has a lot to do with how quickly I *recover*.

It's natural to take a moment to reflect on where things went wrong or what went right, but don't live there. If you want to develop resilience, shift your focus back to your *goal*. Get back to your purpose, to the why. The why is what really matters. Focusing on your *purpose* is what will keep you motivated to get back up and begin again.

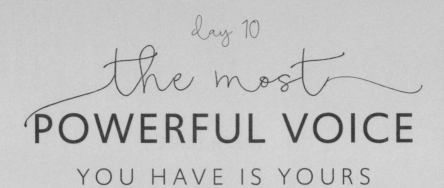

day 10

the most POWERFUL VOICE

YOU HAVE IS YOURS

So many of us spend our lives running around in circles worrying about what people think or say about us. We worry about the judgments they make on our lives.

Instead, *focus* on your own voice and what it's saying to your soul.

Negative self-talk is more damaging than anything anyone else can say to us. Yes, people can hurt our feelings with their words, but we hurt ourselves much more. We must be careful not to repeat someone else's negative narrative inside our own minds. Let their opinion stay just that. Their words can only become a

reality when we *internalize* their negativity and allow it to become our truth.

Your words are a *powerful* resource for your life. Be mindful of speaking negatively about yourself. Your mind hears everything you say and immediately starts working to align your *life* with your words. Continuously calling yourself dumb or fat is only going to create those circumstances in your life.

Don't pay attention to what anyone else says about you. The only *voice* you need to listen to is your own.

day 11

YOU CAN
DO ANYTHING.
NO REALLY, YOU CAN.

What an **exciting** time to be a woman. We are living in an age of great change. Women are reaching **new heights** in all areas of life. Everyday women leave their mark on the world. I think one of them should be you.

We have the **potential** to affect the world even more powerfully if we women could do these two things: rally around and encourage one another. If we support each other's **dreams** despite our differences—instead of focusing on them—we could rise above the media montage of what it means to be a woman. We could make a **real difference.** Isn't that what most of us want?

What are the ideas, dreams, and **passions** you've kept hidden in your heart? Act on them! It doesn't matter how big or difficult they may seem. It's **your turn**.

Everyday women *leave their mark* on the world.   I think *one of them* should be *you*.

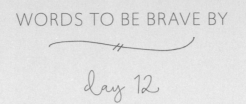
BRAVERY

DOESN'T COME FROM

BEAUTIFUL PLACES.

BRAVERY IS BIRTHED IN

DARK DAYS

AND **UNCERTAINTY**.

Say No

day 13

LEARNING TO SAY NO

I am the worst when it comes to saying no. Not just because I'm a natural-born people pleaser, but also because I *genuinely* want to participate in life and help a friend when I can.

The problem is that participating in everything ends up leaving me time for nothing. Nothing I care about, anyway. I will be busy, but not *productive*. All that busyness just leaves me tired and cranky with no energy left for the people and ideas that *move me*.

This is your reminder that it's okay to say no. It's *more than okay*, it's a requirement. Politely decline an event, a request, or a call at least once a week. Consider it an exercise in becoming comfortable and *confident* at saying no.

You can't do everything at once. There will be times when you say no to things you *love* and yes to things you don't. That's *okay*, too.

PURSUE EXCELLENCE

WHEN YOU'RE GENUINELY TRYING
TO DO YOUR BEST, YOU'RE EXPANDING
WHAT YOUR BEST CAN BE.

day 14

EXCELLENCE

There is power in living a life of excellence. Not under the pressure of **perfection** but in the pursuit of excellence. "Doing your best" seems to be a dying concept these days. The truth is, as adults, we know not everyone gets a trophy, and excellence is required to **succeed**.

Whatever your goal or dream, it requires that you do your very best to achieve it. Dream chasing is not for the halfhearted. It requires epic proportions of **diligence** and tenacity. You must bring your best self to the table.

Pursuing excellence simply means you are working hard at doing your best. I'm not advocating killing yourself for your job or **dream**. Long-term exhaustion isn't productive. I do believe that the earth and the people in it respond positively to those folks who are sincerely doing their best.

I firmly believe that being your truest, most authentic self is a high and moral **calling**, but unearthing that higher self requires intention and work.

Pursue excellence in your self-care, your **relationships**, and your work. When you're genuinely trying to do your best, you're expanding what your best can be. **It grows with you**.

day 15

RISK

Be daring, be brave. Rise above the chatter, and live your life with purpose and passion. Go beyond what most would consider normal. Pursue the extraordinary.

Give yourself permission to chase your dreams in a daring way. Be audacious. There is always risk in growth. No one has ever accomplished anything great by playing it safe.

Risk taking is not your enemy, but living your life in the safety zone is. The worst that can happen is your risk not working out. Second worst thing: other people will see it. Neither of these will kill you. I'm living proof.

You may take one hundred risks with ninety-nine failures, but that's not a good enough reason not to live a daring life. There's too much at stake. Your purpose and your impact on others' lives are worth the risk.

So now that you know you won't die from failure, go ahead and pursue your dreams with tenacity.

RISK

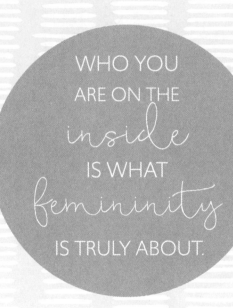

WHO YOU ARE ON THE *inside* IS WHAT *femininity* IS TRULY ABOUT.

day 16

YOUR OWN KIND OF

feminine

LADIES, I'M AFRAID WE'VE BEEN HIJACKED.

The sheer volume of "beauty standards" these days is enough to make one's head spin. Don't get me wrong, I love a good beauty product, but there's more to **beauty** than what we are being fed by the media.

Everywhere we look, we are bombarded with digitally enhanced versions of what it means to be a woman. Femininity has come to mean a certain ideal set by companies selling their product line. The products stoke our **insecurities**, then offer their help. What, your thighs don't look like this model's on the cover of the magazine? We've got a cream for that. That'll be $200, please.

I'm here to tell you that you get to be the creator of your own **femininity**. Want blue hair? Go for it. Want to wear all black for the rest of your life? I'm for you.

Who you are on the inside is what femininity is truly about—not your weight, your clothes, or your hair. You ARE feminine, and you have the chance to **express** it in whatever way you want.

That digitized image cannot compete with the uniquely feminine you. Not even close.

WORDS TO BE BRAVE BY

day 17

Other people's opinions
ARE IRRELEVANT
to your purpose.

Stay the course.

DESIGN YOUR LIFE

for purpose

You're capable of *creating* the life you truly want, a life where you can't wait to get up in the morning just so you can keep taking it all in. Are you unhappy in some area of your life? Then jump in and redesign it. Put yourself on the path of your purpose. Take charge and take action.

Envision what it is you want your life to be like. Keep that vision close to you, and think on it daily. Imagine it. Don't hold back. I give you permission to daydream. You need to be able to see it.

Then get *inspired*. Do what creates joy, what inspires you. You want to feel it. We often neglect doing what makes us feel good. When you feel inspired, you're motivated to make decisions that create a more *passionate*, purposeful life.

Decide to become an active participant in the process of *living* life by your own design. If you don't, the world will fill your life with what it considers important. Be the boss. **DON'T LET ANYONE ELSE DESIGN YOUR LIFE FOR YOU.**

YOU WERE CREATED
TO MANIFEST THE
EXTRAORDINARY.

day 19

UNLOCK YOUR POTENTIAL

Your potential is what you are **capable** of; it's what you have the power to become.

Every person is born with the potential to excel and propel humanity in a **positive** direction. The key is learning to let go of the negativity of your past and dedicate yourself to your future. Surround yourself with people who want to see you succeed.

Commit to a plan, and take as much **action** as you possibly can. When you think you've done all you can, try to do a little more.

Potential has the tendency to surface in the form of talent. Mix that talent with **determination** and hard work, and you have the making of an exceptional life. You were created to manifest the **extraordinary**. As you unlock your potential, you can also help others do the same.

Not Always Nice

day 20

I DON'T KNOW ABOUT YOU,

but I was raised to be a *nice girl*.

I'm grateful for that, but at times I think this also hinders me. While I believe the world could use nicer people, I also think women can miss out on life in the name of being *nice*.

Nice shouldn't come at the expense of your voice or your dreams. Nice doesn't push you to be small or to hide. *Nice* isn't living a joyless life to appease the expectations of others.

Nice can masquerade as people pleasing, but they are not the same thing. Being *nice* to someone comes from generosity and the connection of human exchange—it acknowledges the other person's value. Its source is love. People pleasing, on the other hand, is fear based. It forces you to behave a certain way to avoid conflict.

There are times when being *nice* is the right thing to do. But nice should never come at the expense of your own voice. Learn to be *nice* to yourself by recognizing what *nice* truly means.

day 21

speak up

We've all been there, wanting to **speak up** and share our ideas, but instead we shrink back. Out of fear, we silence ourselves without a second thought. The problem is that our voices and thoughts **deserve** to be heard. They have value.

What are we afraid of? We worry about being judged or being **liked**. We all want the approval of others. There is no shame in that. It's in our DNA to want to stay **connected** to the group.

This fear isn't irrational. Most of us can remember a time when we were rejected or criticized for voicing our opinion. For some reason, that type of rejection seems to stick around, **training** us over and over again to maintain the status quo. Nobody wants to live through that again, so we play it safe and keep quiet.

We have no control over what other people think about us, not really. People will think what they want, but you can't let that silence you. Have the **confidence** to speak up. Don't let fear keep you from using your voice.

DON'T LET
FEAR
KEEP YOU FROM
USING YOUR
VOICE.

YOU
ARE
ALLOWED
TO
CHANGE

day 22

YOU ARE ALLOWED TO CHANGE

Just because you've started down one path doesn't mean you have to stay there. You have options. When you can't change your circumstances, you can change yourself.

Growing, adapting, and changing are all part of the journey. You are not required to stay in the starting position. You are allowed to change your mind and shift your beliefs. As a matter of fact, I hope you do.

Events can occur in life that instantly alter you. Some of them are tragic, and some of them are glorious. Experiencing the birth of a child can transform your life forever, as can the death of a parent.

You do not have to go back to the person you were prior to those moments. I'm uncertain if that's even possible.

At times we need healing, but sometimes the change is so deep that it brings about growth instead. It catapults you forward to a more empathetic, humble version of yourself.

Give yourself permission to be the you that you are right now, at this very moment, all of it. Whether you are rejoicing, grieving, or surviving, live fully in your story. Don't hold back.

day 23

you make
A DIFFERENCE

YES, YOU DO. The good things you do for others don't go unseen.

Take heart, *dear friend*.

Everyone is born with a job to do and a space to fill. Your contribution is vital, whether it's at home, work, or wherever you've been planted. The space you fill and the lives you touch wouldn't be the same if you weren't here living out your *purpose*.

You may not be breaking records or ending world poverty, but your day-to-day life impacts others. The building blocks

of change are kind words to strangers and phone calls to friends in need. It starts with you. What you do *matters*.

Some days you'll feel as though nothing you do makes a difference. That idea couldn't be further from the truth.

The good you do will come back to you. Give generously of *yourself* to those people in your life that you've been joined to.

Keep a "giving goals" journal. Make note of some special ways you would like to *increase* your impact.

day 24

YOUR

uniqueness

is a sacred thing.

HONOR IT.

CULTIVATING
YOUR PLAN

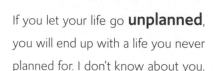

If you let your life go **unplanned**, you will end up with a life you never planned for. I don't know about you, but that isn't what I want.

Your goal begins with your **vision** for your life. Where do you want to go? Who do you want to be? What is it you want to accomplish?

The vision will change and grow as you do.

After determining what you want, set some **goals**. Goals are going to be your new BFF. Keep them in front of you daily. Devote yourself to them.

Your goals will require a plan of action. What do you need to do to reach them? Make a list of things you can do to start building **momentum** toward your goals.

Every day you should be reviewing your goals and the actions you need to take. Don't let a single day go by without taking at least one action that will get you there. This requires a **commitment** to yourself. Your goal needs to become a priority.

Having a plan allows you to adjust your aim and reach your **target**. It's the trajectory.

Nothing **notable** happens without action. We can plan and dream all day long, but in the end, all that matters are the actions we take.

GOALS

ARE GOING TO BE
YOUR NEW

BFF.

Begin Again

Day 26

BEGIN AGAIN

You may experience a time when you are forced to bury something that was *meaningful* to you and start over. Whether it's the loss of a marriage, a relationship, or a job, these times can leave you reeling with feelings of confusion, grief, and a hefty dose of what-ifs.

In the face of uncertainty, you will have to *dig deep* inside yourself and summon up your biggest brave. You'll need to go all in. Don't get stalled while looking for the answer to the question "Why?" You may never know.

Focus on your new beginning. See it as an opportunity to create something new and beautiful in your life. It may be different from the one you had, but it can still be good. You will find happiness again.

As long as you are alive, there is *hope*. You can still fulfill your life's purpose.

day 27

own your
ENERGY

POSSESS IT. GUARD IT. DIRECT IT.

Your precious life's *energy* is something you will have to protect from now until you take your last breath.

Beware of the energy suckers of negativity, self-doubt, and complacency. You will have *relationships* that zap your energy and hinder your motivation. Avoid those at all costs.

Focus your energy on what it takes to accomplish your goals and to live a life of purpose.

The funny thing is, the more you focus your energy on what really *ignites* your passion, the more energy it returns to you, propelling you forward and *upward*.

WHO DO YOU WANT TO BE RIGHT NOW?
TODAY, THIS VERY MOMENT, YOU POSSESS THE CHOICE.

THE LENS OF
THE PAST

The past will haunt you if you let it. It will hover over your present and your **future** like a dark cloud blurring the way to live a successful life.

The truth is the past has no power over your future, not if you don't let it. You can't change what has happened, but you can choose how you will move **forward** despite it.

When we're unable to let go of the past, we become its prisoner, shackled to old wounds and old mind-sets. We carry it around, afraid to part with stories we've told ourselves. We can find **comfort** in those stories because they provide us an answer to the why, but that doesn't mean we need to reread them over and over again.

The past doesn't have to be a life sentence served at the cost of your **peace** now and your success in the future. You can move forward.

Right now is all that matters. Who do you want to be right now? Today, this very moment, you possess the **choice**.

day 29

DON'T DESTROY A PICASSO
BECAUSE IT ISN'T A
MONA LISA

Comparison is a confidence killer. Every one of us is *gifted*, capable, and unique. When we compare ourselves to others, we're not valuing who we are. We exaggerate what we think are our weaknesses and focus on our perceived deficiency.

Spending time *comparing* ourselves to someone else is one way to ensure we never reach our full potential. It's impossible. Our focus is in the wrong place.

Social media can paint pretty pictures, but it shouldn't be where we go to judge our lives. We live in a digitally enhanced world so it's easy to get lost in the "perfection" of it all.

When you see another person doing well in an area of life, you're seeing only one part of her. You don't know what's going on in the rest of her life. You aren't seeing what it took to get there, what *sacrifices* she made.

That's her thing, her slice of *awesome*. You have your own. Keep your focus there.

The path of your life is *unique* to you just as your gifts and purpose are your own. You can't develop your own talents while you're focused on someone else's.

When we COMPARE OURSELVES to others, we're not VALUING WHO WE ARE.

day 30

BE BRAVE ENOUGH
TO MAKE CHOICES **THAT LEAD YOU** OUT OF YOUR **COMFORT ZONE.**

Self-Awareness

day 31

SELF-AWARENESS

I cannot stress enough the importance of being self-aware. You are the most *influential* person in your life. It's vital that you know who you really are and who you want to be.

If you aren't aware of your strengths and weaknesses, then you, my friend, are flying blind. Having that knowledge is essential to *achieving* your goals and creating the life of your dreams. This doesn't mean that you should go about obsessing over your weaknesses or bragging on your strengths. Self-awareness is being *humbly* aware of what areas in your life you can spend time developing and which areas will see you to great achievement.

It's important that we try to improve our weaker areas, everyone knows that. But it shouldn't be the place we spend most of our time and efforts.

Taking time to develop your natural talents should be a *priority*. Work on those things you're good at and make them even better. That's how experts are made. The greatest musicians and artists wouldn't exist if they hadn't been *determined* to dive in and cultivate their craft. Make time to cultivate your own gifts.

Knowing your weaknesses and your strengths is a sign of *maturity*. Spend time in introspection and then write down ways you could improve on both.

IT'S
YOUR
TIME

IT'S YOUR TIME

Time management is a topic that we're all familiar with. For me, I'm hyperaware of time and my lack of control over it. I struggle daily with getting the **important** things done without ignoring the necessary daily tasks.

Time is the great nonrenewable resource. We can't get it back after we've spent it, and I've never met anyone who didn't want more of it. It's an equalizer—we all get the same amount every day until our time is up.

Meeting goals and living your dream life require employing an effective way to manage your time. Without this skill, you'll be tossed around by the demands of daily life, and you'll accomplish less than you hoped for.

This requires that your goals, and the actions needed to accomplish them, become the daily **priority**.

Are you running your day or is your day running you?

Those who **accomplish** great things manage their time. Make it a habit to write down your goals and plan for the day. It's much easier to stay the course when the plan is right in front of you.

day 33

blame

When things aren't working out the way we had hoped, it's easy to look around for someone or something else to blame. If we feel bad, it can't be our fault. Right?

Much of our life is the *culmination* of the choices we've made and actions we've taken. We get back what we put out. Of course, some situations are out of our control, such as being the victim of abuse. Those things are certainly out of the scope of our control. I'm talking about taking responsibility for the way our lives are or aren't *working*.

Even if someone has wronged you with their actions, you are not required to let that be a *defining* moment in your life. You don't have to turn over the reins that control your life because of someone else's bad choices.

Please don't waste months or years blaming someone else for your circumstances. Blaming others turns over the power of your life to someone else. Even if another person's actions did negatively impact you, *forgive* them. Release the blame. It will be much easier to move forward when you take responsibility for your future.

Take some time to reflect and figure out ways to *improve* and move forward.

Your future is created by the choices you make today. Don't contaminate what is to come by looking for somewhere to place the blame if it isn't what you hoped for. Start by taking responsibility for your *future* today.

YOUR
FUTURE
IS CREATED BY THE
CHOICES
YOU MAKE TODAY.

day 34

DISTRACTION
LEADS TO DESTRUCTION . . . OR AT LEAST
MILD DISSATISFACTION

Modern life is full of distractions. On any given day, each of us is presented with an endless supply of **opportunities** and challenges that are vying for our attention and our time. It's endless. Technology has compounded this predicament by giving us a pocket-sized, carry-on distraction device.

I have found that anytime I set myself toward achieving a new goal, I have plenty of distractions to keep me off task.

The **distractions** in life are not the important things, like your spouse or children. Distractions are small things masquerading as big things. Just because something wants your time and attention doesn't mean you are required to give it.

You get plenty of opportunities to lose focus or spread yourself too thin, but to achieve your goals, you must learn to **recognize** and deal with the distraction.

This will mean you can't take every phone call or say yes to every lunch invitation with your friends. That's okay. Phone calls and invitations aren't bad, but they keep you distracted.

Weed through daily distractions because you've got a higher goal that's worthy of **discipline**.

judge your
BODY LESS

Congratulations! You've been given a gift. It's unique, priceless, and powerful.

That gift is your body. Embrace it. Treasure it. Be grateful for it; it has a big job to do.

I've never met a woman who hasn't struggled with body image issues at some point in her life. How could we not? We live in a society that encourages dissatisfaction with the very thing that keeps us alive.

When did we decide our bodies weren't **good enough**? When did we start to believe our value came from how we look?

Your body houses the **eternal** you; the you that will live on long after the death of the body. Your thinking, loving, and creative

parts live inside that body, and the people who love you want you to remain inside of it.

It's our job to be a good **steward** of that body. To nourish it and care for it just like we would a child. The world needs you **regardless** of your dress size.

The more you care for your body, the more it can give you in return. **Treasure** your body like the gift that it is.

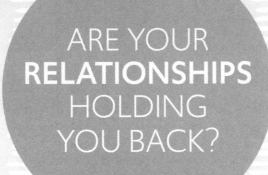

ARE YOUR
RELATIONSHIPS
HOLDING
YOU BACK?

LET STUFF GO

We reach a point in *life* when we must learn to let go of the relationships that are holding us back. Some of the people we started with will not be with us for the long haul. One of the most difficult experiences I've ever gone through was to let go of someone I thought would be by my side for life. It was *difficult*, but I knew I had to do it for us both to grow.

I wouldn't advise tossing people out of your life hastily and without serious consideration. Some people need your *grace* to get past their own issues. Those people, the ones who are sincerely trying, deserve the chance to change. As do you.

Not every ending has to be abrupt and traumatic. You may decide to reduce spending time with them *gradually*, or you can shift the focus of the relationship. For example, if you spend eight hours a week with an old friend, you can reduce it to less than an hour. Or change what you do together and what topics you discuss. Switch it up a bit.

The trouble begins when we hold on to negative relationships that are doing far more damage than any final break ever would. Over time, when the negative effects of a relationship *outweigh* the good, it's time to let go.

Abundance

day 37

Abundance

IN MORE THAN ONE AREA OF YOUR LIFE

Life is not an either/or kind of journey. Don't limit yourself by having a mind-set of scarcity. Let me explain.

We were created to live a full life, with all its rain and sunshine. On our life's journey, we are presented with decisions and options. Just because we experience abundance in one part of our life doesn't justify or warrant lacking in another.

Abundance for you doesn't create a lack for someone else. There is enough goodness in the world for everyone, enough for us to give freely.

The more abundance you have in your life, the more you will have to share with others. Abundant living isn't just about money. Abundant living is having an overflow of joy, humor, love, and kindness. The world is hungry. Share excessively.

Do you have abundant friendships? Bring other people into your circles— expand and include. Do you have an abundance of free time? Volunteer and share your time and attention with those in need. Whatever the area, keep growing and sharing.

day 38

PATIENCE

I'm a "right now" kind of person. Patience is not my *natural* disposition. I want the fast-food version of achievement. I want it instantly, and I want it big. Unfortunately for me, that isn't how life typically works.

With all the planning, praying, and participating, you still may not be *progressing* toward your goals as quickly as you would like. The passage of time comes with the territory of having goals. One of the greatest parts of working toward your goals is the person you become along the way. It's what you learn about yourself and others while you are *pursuing* the dream. Patience is one of those things.

Most folks who have accomplished anything noteworthy would agree that seeing your *dreams* come to pass takes more time and effort than you first anticipated. Inevitably, you will face setbacks and delays, brick walls and burned bridges. That's part of the *process*.

Just because things don't appear to be going as quickly as expected isn't a sign to quit or give up on your dream. It takes time for your dreams to be realized. Make a plan. Do the work. Be *patient*.

MAKE A PLAN.
DO THE WORK. **BE PATIENT.**

YOU'RE PERFECT EVEN WHEN YOU'RE NOT

day 39

YOU'RE PERFECT
EVEN WHEN YOU'RE NOT

One **guaranteed** way to never accomplish anything is to get trapped in the loop of perfectionism.

Perfectionism, that pest. Call it what it is: **insecurity**, fear. Just when you get all hyped-up to put yourself out there and dream big, perfectionism creeps in, sucking the joy out of the process.

I've given up on too many projects to count because I couldn't make them—or myself, rather—perfect. If I perceived some imperfection in my work or creative project, I viewed that as a direct reflection of MY imperfection, thus cutting off my **creativity**. What a shame. Do you do that?

We must give up on the illusion and delusion of perfection. Perfect doesn't exist. It's a **false** ideal. You can photoshop media, but you can't photoshop life. We're in this together, warts and all.

You should never not do something or not create something just because you can't do it perfectly. This applies to dancing, crafting, even loving. When did **perfection** become a requirement?

You are allowed to be imperfect; that's part of being human. You aren't inferior to anything or anyone. Perfection is subjective anyway. Dream big, create, and embrace your **humanity**.

THE DARK SIDE
OF GOSSIP

The older I get, the more important it is for me to remove myself from conversations that revolve around the *misfortune* of others.

From reality television to scathing political battles, the aim is to destroy another individual. There's no privacy and nothing is off-limits. People betray the confidences of their "friends" and stir the *drama* in relentless catfighting.

We live in a culture that feasts on ruining someone else's character. Gossip *destroys* relationships and erodes trust. What our mothers told us is true: if they will talk about others with you, they will talk about you with others.

If we want to empower women, we should start by eradicating gossip from our lives. It's a hurtful mechanism so often used to soothe our own insecurities and self-doubts. We are not *elevated* by verbally putting others down. The act of gossip itself is more damaging to the doer than the object of the ridicule. We know when we've said something we shouldn't have. We hear ourselves, and we know it's not right.

Let's set an *example* by building up someone in the presence of others. Speaking kind words can do more than make another person feel good, it can empower a woman to be *brave*.

Speaking
KIND WORDS
CAN EMPOWER
A WOMAN TO BE
BRAVE.

day 41

YOU DON'T HAVE TO
fight
EVERY FIGHT

I've been preaching this to my children since they exited the womb. I tell them just because someone, namely their sibling, comes at them sideways, they aren't required to participate in the **drama**. More adults should jump on the drama-free bandwagon.

Not every battle that presents itself is worth the **effort** it would take to engage in it.

Social media and the newest technologies make it easier than ever to **engage** in an ugly war of words with a total stranger. People hide behind screens and buttons to challenge everything and everyone in a combat strategy fit for a courtroom.

I'm ever shocked by what people will say to one another and why. We aren't just fighting about politics and moral issues because at least some of those discussions can have **meaning**. As a culture, it seems we're fighting people for no reason at all other than someone looks or lives differently

than we do. Attacks aren't only over ideas, but the person's character. Fights get personal.

Maybe if we disengage with those who challenge every detail of our lives, we could **reap** the reward of more meaningful relationships.

It takes time to argue and fight, not to mention the physical and emotional toll on our bodies.

There are ideas and people worth fighting for, we all know that. But little things can quickly turn into big drama and steal the peace out of our lives—a social media post, a nasty comment by your teenager, a spouse who isn't listening.

The next time someone wants to create drama in your life, save yourself the trouble and **walk away**. Let them keep their chaos. You have more important things to do.

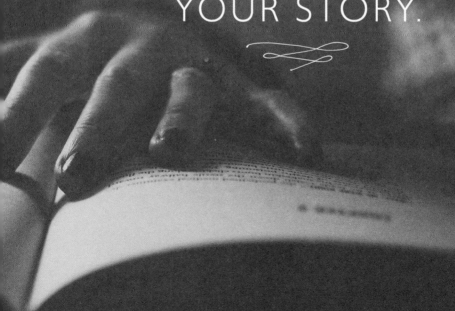

day 42

YOU HAVE THE
POWER
TO CHANGE
YOUR STORY.

Gratitude

day 43

WHY IS *gratitude* SO IMPORTANT?

Gratitude is a mind-altering, game-changing attitude. It's a force so powerful it can change the *chemistry* in your body just by expressing it.

Modern life carries with it a great deal of stress. It's easy to get bogged down by the heaviness of it all.

All the ugliness and heaviness of this world cannot hold a candle to gratitude. A heavy heart and gratitude can't operate at the same time. Gratitude gives you your power back. It *elevates* your thinking and opens the door to peace.

We have an abundance of riches to be thankful for, even if some days we need to look a little harder to find them. I've met many people going through difficult situations who have been able to *practice* gratitude, even in the midst of chaos.

Expressing gratitude is *meditating* on what is good. Making that shift in perspective can change your attitude and your life. Set aside a few minutes daily to write down what you are truly grateful for and then say it aloud. There is something powerful about our minds and our bodies being reminded of all that we have to be *grateful* for. Implement this on your good days and on the days you just want to forget (especially those).

You'll be surprised how much this simple process will change your outlook.

MAKE A HABIT OF CELEBRATING
YOUR ACHIEVEMENTS EVERY DAY.

Day 44

CELEBRATE
YOUR VICTORIES

Do you wallow in your perceived failures? I've been known to do this a time or two. I replay them in my mind's eye again and again, examining every detail, every circumstance leading up to it. It's self-inflicted torture.

But what about our **victories**? Why don't we examine, dissect, and replay those?

If we spent a fraction of the time **celebrating** ourselves as we do rehashing old failures, our lives would drastically change. When we learn to celebrate our victories more than our failures, it will increase our **confidence** and keep us motivated toward reaching our bigger goals.

Trying to lose twenty-five pounds? Celebrate that five-pound loss. Trying to declutter your house? Celebrate that one drawer you cleared out today.

Revel in things done right.

Make a habit of celebrating your **achievements** every day. Tell yourself how awesome you are and how incredible life is. It's the quickest way to lighten up, and most of us could use a little of that.

day 45

YOUR PASSION IS

your gift

TO THE WORLD

Whatever it is that sets your heart on fire, do that, and do it habitually. You do not have to make a job out of your *passion* for it to have a positive effect on your life and those around you. All that is required is that you let your gifts and passions flow through you. *Release* it to be shared with the world. That is where you will make an impact.

I truly believe when you were created, God *endowed* you with something unique, special, and powerful. The problem is that we bury these gifts under fear, stress, and responsibilities. It's time to dig them up, dust them off, and *shine* a light on them.

Nobody benefits when you leave your gifts untouched. It's not only about you, it's about the people who are starving and looking for the light. You can be that light. Are you gifted at baking chocolate chip cookies? (If so, then we should be friends.) Bake away, share, and teach. Whatever it is you can do with those cookies, do it. Take them to a grieving friend, donate them to the community center, just do something with them. It's so important that you do not let your gift lie idle inside of you.

Pour from the vessel you've been given and be refreshed.

Envision YOUR GOALS AGAIN AND AGAIN UNTIL *your energy* IS RENEWED.

day 46
there will be
THOSE DAYS

We've all experienced them . . . those days when it feels like you can't take one more step. When the *weight* of it all is too much. I call those the days of overwhelm. It's hard to accomplish anything with feelings of defeat choking out your motivation.

When those days of overwhelm pop in for a visit, find a way back to your core.

Why are you here? What do you truly want? *Meditate* on that. If you can reconnect with your passion, you can pull yourself up and keep going.

Focus on your goals, not the difficulties. Hard times will pass. I'm not telling you to stick your head in the sand and pretend everything is perfect. Denying reality is rarely wise, but you can *shift* your focus to something productive and positive. You aren't ignoring your problems, you're changing your focus. Rise higher and get a better point of view. That's the game changer.

Envision your goals again and again until your energy is renewed.

Whether it's weight loss, job change, or moving to a new place, don't give up.

NO ONE
GETS TO
TELL YOU

day 47

NO ONE
GETS TO TELL YOU

No one has the **power** to decide who you are going to be in this life.

The good news is you get to choose. **Yes, you do.** You choose daily, minute by minute. Even your smallest choices are shaping and creating your life in the now and for the future.

Don't allow yourself to be pigeonholed by your past or by how others view you.

As you try to make **positive** changes and advance your life, you'll encounter people who are chained to their old perspective of you. They can't embrace your newfound you-ness. Don't let anyone else's outdated mind-set keep you from living out the fullness of who you hope to become.

No matter where you come from, what you've done, how little or how much education you've received. Nobody gets to **decide** who you are. You are completely under your own design.

Allowing other people's ideas to form the narrative of your life is a disservice to your purpose. Take **advantage** of the power you've been given to decide who you want to be and how you want to live.

Raise Your Standards

day 48

RAISE
YOUR STANDARDS

Dear girl, I mean that. There comes a time when you need to raise the *standards* of your relationships. Don't let someone stay in your life if that person doesn't have your best interest at heart.

When I think of standards, I think of *boundaries*. Whether we're establishing boundaries for ourselves or boundaries in our relationships, we need healthy ones, big, mighty, well-defined ones.

We have no control over the *actions* of others, but we do have power over how we let their actions affect our lives. The people in our lives should bring us joy, love, and some sense of peace—not constant chaos.

It starts with you and how well you *love* yourself. When you are loving yourself properly, it sets the standard for the other relationships in your life.

Too often we allow other people's toxic behavior to drain our lives of joy and peace. It shouldn't be so.

Raise your standards for who you let into your inner circle.

day 49

you are

WORTHY

You are worthy of every **good** and **precious** gift. The first time I said this to myself, I literally cringed. Speaking kind words to myself always makes me uncomfortable at first. I wish it didn't.

Humans struggle to accept feeling worthy of goodness. It's as though we are hardwired to be uncertain of our ability to give and receive **abundance**. Abundance, by definition, is more than what is needed; it's enough to share. We were **created** with an abundant purpose, a purpose that enhances our lives as well as the lives of others. Abundance spills over the edges.

You are **worthy** of giving and receiving all the goodness this world has to offer, even when you think you aren't enough. There is nothing so greatly lacking within you that it disqualifies you from being worthy of abundance. Doubting your worth will sabotage your **goals**.

You **deserve** to be healthy. You deserve to have an abundance of love and grace and kindness. You deserve to experience the **goodness** of life.

Believe in your own worthiness, and open yourself up to receive the abundant life you were **created** to live.

BELIEVE IN YOUR
OWN WORTHINESS.

day 50

FEMALE
friendships

Female relationships can be *complex* and intense. What happens when one of those trusted women abandons your friendship? What if you never fully know why? For many women, the loss of a female friend is just as intense as losing a loved one.

How do we go about *recovering* when the trust in a friendship is broken? Of course, you forgive them and yourself, but after that? Relationships can reach a point of being so damaged that no matter how much you forgive each other, the relationship is irreparable. Sometimes the other person isn't interested in repairing it anyway.

Then you are left with a void where *trust* used to reside. That stings.

When you think you know someone, and years later you find out you don't, it can cause you to doubt yourself. Betrayal from someone you trusted can make you question your instincts and your heart. You might ask yourself, *How did I not see this coming? Was it even real? What sign did I miss?*

I know it isn't easy, but you must let go of the what-ifs and move *forward* in your life. Forgive yourself for not recognizing the problem before it blew up in your face. For your own good, let that person go even when your side deserves to be heard. You may never fully understand why the relationship ended. Sometimes we don't get the answers we're so hungry for. That's just part of it.

You can't spend your *precious* life energy continually mourning the loss of a relationship. Yes, it hurt, but it doesn't have to hurt forever.

The world is full of people who want to be in your life. Almost every woman I know is actively looking for new *friendships*.

You will *survive* the loss. You will form new relationships. Don't lose hope.

day 51

DO NOT WAIT
FOR THE
ABSENCE OF FEAR.
BE BRAVE.
STEP OUT IN
faith.

GRIT

Fulfilling your purpose won't be easy. Not at all.

The road to living out your **destiny** will be paved with obstacles, setbacks, and disappointments. Count on it.

No matter who you are or how worthy your endeavor, you're going to need some grit to accomplish it.

What is grit? Grit is **resolve**. It's hanging on when you feel like letting go. It's the courage to go through the hard stuff.

I've learned two important lessons in my journey toward accomplishing my dreams.

One, I had to **commit** myself to the process. I had to keep showing up. And two, I didn't need to be **perfect**. I only needed to know how to keep getting back up. Grit is committed determination.

Somewhere along the way we bought into the illusion that if we were **destined** to have it, then it would be easy to get it. Oh, and it would be wrapped up with a tidy red bow on our doorstep. No wonder we get discouraged at the first sign of resistance.

Everything you want to **accomplish** will require repeated effort and determination. You'll have to dig deep to find it, but bring out your grit. It really is the **secret** to success.

GRIT
IS COMMITTED
DETERMINATION.

HABITS
BUILD
YOUR
LIFE

day 53

HABITS
BUILD YOUR LIFE

Your life is designed by the choices you make every day. Even the small decisions have impact.

Your habits, the things you do every day, are the building blocks of your life. The small **actions** taken daily bring structure to your life and will help you meet your goals.

There are times when a dramatic turn of events can usher you into the middle of your **purpose**. It's the daily choices and constructive habits that will have prepared you to jump at the opportunity, prepared and eager. Habits are choices in training that are **steering** your life toward your goals.

Make sure your daily routine is setting you up to achieve your goals and moving you toward fulfilling your truest **purpose**. Dedicate time in each day to envision what it is you hope to accomplish. Work your plan, even if it's just a little bit each day or week. Remember, small, consistent steps will lead to you crushing your goals later.

Consistency in your habits is a **building block** for achievement.

Choosing Joy

day 54

CHOOSING JOY

That's a tall order: taking *responsibility* for the joy in your life. It makes me cringe just thinking about the many times I've turned over my joy to others to navigate for me.

Whether or not we live a life of joy is a choice we make. You own the rights to your *joy*. Nobody else has that power unless you give it to them. Even then, no one else can create a joyful life for you. It doesn't work. Other people's narrative for joy won't work in your own life.

You can build a life of joy by *deciding* today to let go of what's weighing you down.

Forgive who you need to forgive, including yourself. Take time to do those activities that refresh your *spirit*. Learn to say no without guilt. Express gratitude for your life and the people in it. Love your people and your pets. All these things can increase your joy.

I've lost a lot of joy in my life by focusing my thoughts and energy on what's wrong instead of what is right.

The fastest way to a joyful life is to take on the responsibility of *creating* one. Own it.

NOTHING GOOD COMES FROM
DIMINISHING YOURSELF. *EVER.*

MAKING YOUR LIFE SMALL
DOESN'T MAKE
THE WORLD A LESS SCARY PLACE

Most of my life I tried to keep my life on the small side. This included my body, my career, and my circle of friends. I was afraid. At the core of this belief was the thought that if I kept everything small, then the world wouldn't notice me, and maybe I could make it through this life unscathed. I was intimidated by the idea of my own **success**. Stay small and stay safe.

Wow, was I wrong.

Maybe all my efforts at keeping my life small would have been better served instead by making them authentic and **purposeful**. I've wasted a good portion of my life feeding the delusion that there was safety in not being seen. The more I tried to hide, the more frustrated I felt. The problem with hiding and playing small is that it isn't authentic to who I am. I wanted to have a bigger impact on this world.

We cannot live **authentically** when we are constantly diminishing ourselves. Nothing good comes from diminishing yourself. Ever.

Do you have parts of your life you've kept small even when you knew you were destined for more? Destined for a life of **impact**?

Give yourself permission to envision the bigness of the life you feel inside of you. Living your life small doesn't keep you safe. It keeps you from living the truth you were created to be on this earth. Living the big life you feel inside of you isn't about being famous, it's about having an impact on this world. It's about bringing goodness and change in the sphere of influence you've been given.

There is no safety in being **invisible**. That's faulty reasoning. You were not created to be invisible. **FREE YOURSELF TO DREAM BIG!**

day 56

IT'S NOT

failure

IF YOU LEARNED FROM IT

We've all been there. We planned, we set goals, we took action, and then *suddenly* it all fell apart. Right there in front of us is a scorched remnant pile of our dreams. That's not what we thought would happen.

This is a defining moment for most of us. Do we get back up and try again? Or do we somehow interpret this failure as a sign that we never should have dared to try anyway?

People who reach their goals and *achieve* their dreams do the former. They pull themselves up as best they can, although it might not be pretty, and they continue. The word *quit* isn't in their vocabulary.

Those failures, if they can even be called that, bring clarity to our *vision* and strategies. Just because one try at achieving a goal didn't work out, that doesn't mean you shouldn't have even tried.

I've always imagined it as *building* a bridge to my dreams. Just because one storm comes and blows away the construction, doesn't mean I don't still

want to build the bridge. Instead, I adjust my plans, but the goal remains the same. Next time, I will build it back *stronger* than before.

Think about all the great modern-day necessities that wouldn't exist if people had given up after one failure, or three, or even a hundred, for that matter.

We would never cure diseases. Never create masterpieces. Never know the *comfort* of lasting love.

Better to fail while taking a risk than to sit on the sideline never risking anything because of fear. Keep picking yourself up. Keep moving ahead. It will be worth it.

Yes, you will have disappointments. That's okay. It's not over until you quit *trying*. Don't ever quit.

day 57

MAKE CHOICES
YOUR FUTURE SELF
will thank you for

It's easy to get caught up in the moment and make choices that aren't what's best for your future.

Goals are not achieved some day far off on the horizon; they are achieved in the now. This very minute you are making choices that will either take you where you want to go or will hinder you.

You can apply this to every area of your life. Trying to get *healthy* or save money to buy a home? Maybe you're trying to go back to school because you want to finish that degree you started. Regardless of your situation, becoming who you want to be will require planning and action. You *choose* your way to the life you want.

The pain of *surrendering* to the right choice now will certainly be less painful than the pain of never reaching our goals. Wouldn't you rather face a little discomfort now if it helped you become the person you want to be?

Value your body. Value your future. Value the *opportunities* you've been given. Make choices that reflect those values, and your future self will thank you.

VALUE THE
OPPORTUNITIES
YOU'VE BEEN
GIVEN.

LET GO OF REGRET

LET GO OF
REGRET

Letting go of regret is the **forgiveness** we give to ourselves.

Let's face it, no one is making it out of this life in the same pristine condition that they entered it. You and I have both made mistakes over the years. Some mistakes were major, some of them jaw-dropping (I'm speaking from experience on that one).

As if the mistake alone wasn't enough to bring us down, we **prolong** its impact by keeping it alive long after the consequences have faded. We replay it faithfully and, in doing so, tear down our self-confidence with every outtake.

Let go of regret. **Forgive yourself.** Be free.

Everyone makes mistakes. Everyone. No one has the right to judge you, so stop judging yourself and move on with your life.

Regret is a heavy load. I hate that "if only" feeling. The past can't be changed. Trust me, I've checked. All we can do is forgive ourselves for not being perfect, for not knowing everything all the time, and then **release** that burden.

Lack AND ITS Lies

day 59

LACK AND ITS LIES

Have you ever had a personal revelation burst onto the scene, bringing with it all types of disruption? Not all disruption is bad; some of it can save your life.

This happened to me recently, and it has opened up a whole new string of *questions* for me.

Lack is one of those things I thought I had dealt with. I thought I had outgrown it. Obviously not.

One day while I was out walking, I realized how everything I thought I lacked and how I was perceived because of it were still *deeply* entrenched in my thinking.

When I began to reflect on my life, I realized I spent an awful lot of it trying to cover what I felt I lacked: my lack of people skills, my lack of friends, my lack of confidence. I believe I lacked these things because I was lacking as a person.

There's a lot of history here. I won't go into some of it right now.

But I can tell you that I learned early on I was not enough. I was different, and different was bad. I felt my deficiencies deeply, and I always felt they were branded on my forehead for everyone else to see. Those *feelings* of lack fostered shame.

On to being a thinking adult, wife, and mother, I dealt with those feelings and worked diligently to move past the lie. I told myself that I was enough. I was not wrong. I had been made *whole*.

The problem is that sometimes those feelings of lack need to be dealt with in layers. We can't handle it all at once, so it comes up at different times during our *spiritual* growth.

We peel back layer by layer to uncover the truth, the truth that there is no lack.

day 60

I'M NOT ASKING YOU TO
BUILD A ROCKET SHIP

I'm asking you to take the first step toward your **goal**. Move yourself in the direction of your dreams. Taking action is the number one thing you can do to propel your life forward in a positive, purposeful way.

Some days it will be more work than others. Some days progress will be easy. Some days not so much. On those days, you will want to **quit**, to give up on yourself and your dreams.

Just take another step. Then another. **Overcome** the inertia of complacency. A body in motion stays in motion.

This is the difference between those who reach their goals and those who do not.

Don't let **feelings** drive your actions. It's about determination. It's about committing to your decision. Then give it everything you've got.

Don't leave yourself any other **options**.

EXIT

UNITED STATES

Move yourself IN THE DIRECTION OF YOUR **DREAMS.**

day 61

THE DAYS

go by fast

I wish I had known this when I was younger. I was so busy with two little children, managing a home, and building a business that I let a lot of things slip through my fingers. Don't get me wrong, I didn't do it all wrong, but I could have paid closer attention to the **deeper** things.

While I was busy scrubbing my floors to perfection, the world was passing me by.

With the constant demands of daily life, it's easy to go into autopilot mode and become entangled in less important things. There's a tendency in life to move from task to task without any sense of **focus**. It's a revolving door of things we think we need to do. Instead, maybe we should **slow down** for a minute and set ourselves to live intentionally.

It's so clear now that my children have grown and moved off to college. All the moments I spent in such a hurry and so **overwhelmed** by my lack of perfection, I can't get back. I want to talk to my younger self and tell her to chill a little bit. She's doing all right. Breathe.

It's not just about taking care of our families, it's about enjoying them as well. Whether our obligations are to work, school, or family and friends, make time to really **notice** these people and moments that make up a large portion of our lives.

Be **mindful** of the days because, before you know it, the years will have gone by. Live for the small joys and **celebrate** small victories. Notice them all. Take it in. It's the sum of your life.

day 62

YOU DON'T HAVE TO BE
BULLETPROOF
TO TAKE A
LEAP OF FAITH
YOU NEED ONLY TO BE
BRAVE.

day 63

OWNING *your* JOURNEY

When we are young, it's so easy to look to the future and *believe* that it's only a matter of time before we are plopped down in the middle of our purpose with goals in hand and lots of laughter along the way.

As *time* goes on and disappointment sets in, some of the faith we had in finding our purpose begins to wane. We haven't reached our goals, not even close. Life is harder than we thought. It takes so much more effort to accomplish anything that we can begin to think we'll never get there.

I reached a point in my own life when I woke up one morning and *wondered* if there was anything left for me. Here I was over forty, an empty nester, and feeling all-around miserable, wondering what I could possibly contribute to this world.

I had let so much of myself die, or so I'd thought. It was buried underneath years of PTA meetings, sporting events, and laundry. So much laundry.

My *feelings* were not my family's problem. I had to own this. This was about me taking the easier path, the path of least resistance. My lack of pursuing my goals is not my children's nor my husband's burden to carry. This was on me.

I had justified my lack of faith and follow-through with *family* responsibilities, but the truth is there are lots of folks with families who don't give up on themselves.

I kept *wondering* if it was too late.

Most people think there is only one path, and if you miss that path, then you're in deep trouble.

That's not how I see life now. To me, life is more like a tree. The trunk is the path, and there are many *branches*. Sometimes we branch out in the wrong direction, but there's always the opportunity to get back to the path, even if it takes some *time*.

DON'T LET
THE
DIFFICULTIES
OF LIFE
HARDEN
YOUR HEART

Day 64

DON'T LET THE
DIFFICULTIES OF LIFE
HARDEN YOUR HEART

It's easy to fall into the trap of walling ourselves off from people, **opportunities**, and experiences.

We get hurt, or we go through hard times, and we begin to guard parts of our hearts. We guard ourselves for protection, but the same mechanism that protects us from pain also keeps out more positive emotions like love and joy. That hardness, those walls we've so carefully constructed, will keep us **trapped** inside of ourselves, unable to find the human connection we are so hungry for.

I believe this hardness is caused by fear and a lack of **forgiveness**. We harbor these toxic emotions, befriend them, and use their lies as bricks around our hearts.

Protecting is easier than forgiving. Thankfully, we aren't the types to look for the easy way out.

Even when it isn't easy, we should try to **forgive** as quickly as possible. We forgive so we can experience joy once again and so we're open to meeting new people.

People in this world right now are looking for your exact expression of light. Don't remain behind a wall. Forgive and shine.

Motivated Much?

day 65

MOTIVATED MUCH?

If you want to get anywhere in this life, you will have to learn how to stay **motivated**. Sure, it's easy at the takeoff; the energy and excitement are high. But what happens when you hit a wall or fall off a bridge? Metaphorically, of course.

You will need motivation to get back up and start chipping away again.

It's nice to have friends, family, or speakers who encourage you, but they can't get inside of your brain and change your will. **External** motivation only helps in the short-term, but lasting motivation comes from within you. Without an internal drive, your goals will gather dust and soon be forgotten.

Here is where your **why** comes in. Why are you charting this course? What motivated you to begin with? The purpose must be strong and personal. Most of the time, this type of deep motivation comes from **believing** in something bigger than yourself. What do you believe in? Superficial things are cheap motivators that don't last, but motivation that comes from wanting to positively impact the world can **fuel** you for a lifetime.

Your why will motivate you when you feel like you can't take another step. Your why, your belief about why you are doing what you are doing, will stay with you day and night until you see your dreams come to pass and your mission **accomplished**..

day 66

CULTIVATING BELIEF *in yourself*

I used to think that you were either born **confident** or you weren't. It looked so easy for some people to pop up, grab life by the horns, and ride it to their destiny. I am not one of those people. I wish I were.

I have had to develop the skill of believing in myself. It's something I still work on daily.

Believing in yourself starts with giving yourself **permission** to do that very thing. Believe. It begins with a choice. Look in the mirror, and affirm your God-given abilities. Choose to stop the negative self-talk, choose what you put in your mind. Don't let the old negative narratives play on a loop inside your brain. I hate those loops.

You can **cultivate** confidence. Get up in the morning, show up for your life dressed and ready. Do those things that build you up. Exercise, volunteer, sing, do whatever makes you feel good about being you, and then do it some more.

If there are areas of your life that make you feel less confident, tackle those first, if they are in your control. Just the act of improving your life and taking back control over an undisciplined area will give a much-needed confidence boost.

Focus on what you can accomplish and watch your confidence grow in epic proportions. Show some gratitude for your gifts. You've got them. Share them and watch how your gifts help others. Inspire and be inspired.

day 67

KEEPING UP

appearances

I'm going to talk about a sensitive topic. Our appearance.

I know for us as women, this topic can be misconstrued or diverted and can turn to talk of *vanity* or feminism (what to wear, what not to wear, and why). So, it's important to put the value on appearance in the right light.

It matters how we look. But I'm not talking about weight or body type. I'm not talking about chest size or the size of our thighs. I'm not talking about clothing styles or labels.

The idea is to get up in the morning and intentionally decide how you want to *present* yourself to the world on that particular day. Now, we all have days of throwing on sweats and a hat because that's what our soul needs. But more often, it's nourishing to present yourself in such a way that *boosts* your confidence, giving you the freedom to not think about your appearance for the rest of the day.

It can feel terrible to be in a group of people at work or at the kids' school and feel uncomfortable in our skin because we didn't make ourselves a priority that morning—whatever that might mean for each of us.

When I was young and feeling bad, whether ill or just ill-tempered, I would

often lay around the house in my pj's for what was way too long. My mom, after caring for me and putting up with my self-pity for a few days, would tell me to get up, go shower, and put on some clean clothes. She would tell me that I wasn't going to feel any better if I lazed around another day with dirty hair and old pajamas.

I see now she was trying to *teach* me how to stop the pity party I had thrown for myself—to go wash it off, shake it out, and do whatever was necessary to get myself going again. My mom knew when I needed to *reprioritize* and get on with my self-care. She was doing that long before it became trendy.

The truth is, the world *responds* to how we present ourselves. It's vital that we take time to clean up and get dressed. If we are uncomfortable because our clothes aren't clean or we didn't brush our hair, then our discomfort will radiate into the world. When we're not feeling confident, we have a tendency to shy away from new people. We might even miss out on opportunities because our minds are focused elsewhere. A little extra self-care can make a big *difference* in your confidence and the outcomes in your life.

day 68

CREATIVITY IS
GRATITUDE IN ACTION

Don't hand me the "I'm not creative" spiel. I don't buy it. Everyone is **creative**, even if you think you aren't. We were put on this earth to create in one form or another. Whether you're a stay-at-home mom, a teacher, or a CEO, creativity is inside of you. Creativity is not relegated to the artistic few. It's in all of us.

For me, creativity is **gratitude** in motion. God has given each of us gifts; most folks have more than one. When you utilize those gifts and share them with others, you are being creative. Creativity is a form of gratitude because when you're giving back, you're honoring your Creator by using the talents He gave you.

When you are creating, in whatever form that takes, you are manifesting **divinity** here on earth. Maybe you're a teacher thinking of new ideas to help a child who's struggling—that's creativity. Or you could be a nurse trying different ways to lift the **spirit** of a suffering patient—that's creativity.

Express your gratitude by freely giving of your creativity to a hurting world.

Express your
GRATITUDE
BY FREELY GIVING OF
YOUR CREATIVITY
TO A HURTING WORLD.

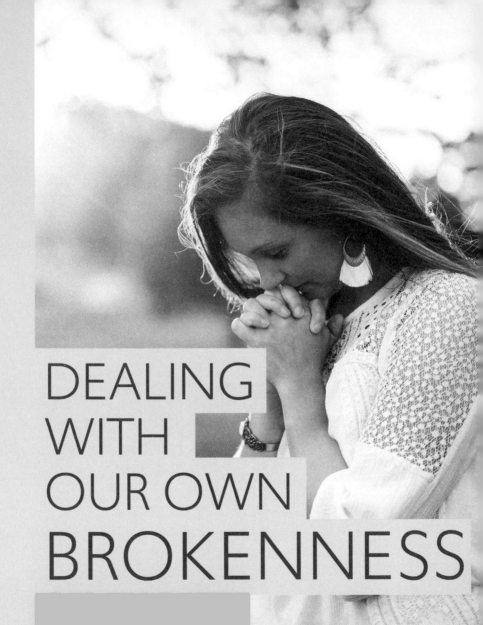

DEALING WITH OUR OWN BROKENNESS

DEALING WITH OUR OWN
BROKENNESS

Not one of us will make it through this life without getting some piece of our hearts broken. That takes many different forms, but it **touches** us all.

Pain is a powerful **motivator**. We will do almost anything to avoid feeling it. We're hardwired to avoid it. On instinct, we protect ourselves from that which could harm us, even if in the end this avoidance actually causes us more pain.

Sometimes we need to just sit with the pain. We **grow** when we face it.

Amazing things can happen when we allow ourselves to sit with the pain. We should stop stuffing down, ignoring, and medicating it. We gorge on food, shopping, web surfing, and a myriad of other distractions. All this **consuming** and no healing.

As long as we avoid the truth of our pain, it will continue causing unwanted side effects.

Healing begins the moment we allow ourselves to feel the pain. Take a deep breath, and look at your brokenness. Don't turn away. Acknowledge it, and begin to view it in a new way. Release it. Feel your **freedom**.

Pain doesn't have to last forever; you CAN heal. Your pain doesn't define you if you don't let it. You deserve to move past the hurt and create a life of **joy**.

Permission

day 70

HOW ABOUT WE GIVE EACH OTHER
PERMISSION
TO BE OURSELVES ENTIRELY

It's okay for you to be you in all your wacky glory. It's okay for you to be extra, every single day.

At some point, you have to give up *seeking* other people's approval, especially if that approval requires that you fundamentally change who you are. Oh, the energy and time wasted while looking for ways to fit in.

You hear it all the time because it's true: *normal* is overrated. Fitting in is overrated. But what does that even mean? Fit in with whom? Fit in how?

Some person—real or imagined—set the status quo on what it means to be a woman or wife or mother or friend or whatever role you find yourselves in. You see that person and think, *Okay, everyone likes her, so I'm going to be like her, and then everyone will like me, too. I will be normal, organized, and stain-free just like she is.*

I just won't let you know about my weird driftwood collection or my childhood obsession with Chia Pets.

The crazy part is, we all want the same thing. Everyone wants to be *accepted* and liked. It's the way we're wired.

Somewhere along the way we were taught that we *needed* to bend and contort ourselves into other, better people in order to belong. That just isn't true.

As women, we need to give each other permission to be our truest selves in front of each other. We need to give each other permission to take off the mask and share our *authentic* selves with our neighbor without fear of rejection and judgment.

day 71
YOU HAVE MORE CONTROL
over your life
THAN YOU KNOW

Many don't agree with me, but this core belief has helped me find some success in this life.

You are to be a *steward* over the life God gave you. That stewardship gives you tremendous control over the outcomes in your life. You are given the opportunity to live your life the way you feel is right. With such an opportunity also comes responsibility.

With the gift of life comes the responsibility for that life. Taking *control* starts with taking responsibility. Yes, that's right. When you take responsibility for every area of your life, you gain greater control over the outcome. It's the opposite of having a victim mentality.

Certainly, life can throw you curveballs and maybe even knock you out. I'm not implying you can stop every negative situation that arises, but you can control how you *respond* to it. You control your next move. You can't control other people, and you can't control those bent on destruction and harm. If we could, there would be much less violence in this world.

You may find comfort in believing you have no control, but it's not the truth. It's easy to succumb to the idea that you aren't responsible for the fulfillment of your purpose, but you are.

This means doing your best. It means taking on the task of living your best life.

It takes faith to accept responsibility for your life. You need to own it. I believe in God, his angels, and in divine appointments. But I also believe God gave us a mind and a mouth for a reason. He expects us to use them for good, so we need to put them to work.

What this means is that hard work, commitment, and excellence really do pay off. Want to be healthier? Take responsibility by exercising and eating properly. Want to improve your relationships? Ask yourself what you're contributing before expecting someone else to do the same. It's about asking yourself, *What can I do to make things better?*

So much is beyond our control, so many terrible possibilities. But I'm not focused there. My faith and my prayer life get a good workout on those topics.

You have control over your attitude. This sets the tone of your life.

You have control over your gratitude. This opens the door for abundance.

So much of your life is up to you. You can choose to take risks, to put yourself out there, and reap the rewards. You can choose gratitude and kindness in a world that forgets such basic human things.

The good news is that you are not powerless. You've been given the opportunity to create a life of purpose and meaning.

day 72

SELF-CARE IS NOT VANITY,
NOT EVEN CLOSE

We often put others' **needs** ahead of our own, believing we will care for ourselves later. Something else pops up and pushes our own needs farther down the list. Too often we put ourselves at the bottom of our priority list, if we make the list at all.

You must make your whole self a **priority**. You hear it all the time, but few actually practice it.

When you practice self-care, you are investing in yourself. The better you feel, the healthier you are, the more attention and focus you can give to the people you love and the purpose you are so passionate about. Even the smallest **investments** can energize and restore you.

You don't want to wake one day and think, *Wow. I'm done. I have nothing left to give.* I'm speaking from experience on this one. I'm sad to admit I have run my body and mind to the point of collapse and wish that for no one.

No one can pour from an **empty** cup. Pushing yourself to physical, mental, and spiritual exhaustion isn't healthy for you, your relationships, or your purpose.

If you need rest, then rest. If you need quiet, then find that quiet space. If you need exercise, get moving. If you need time alone, then spend time alone without **guilt**.

It's not always easy to do when you have so much vying for your attention. All those daily responsibilities can make it feel impossible, but I **promise** you, it's not. It takes discipline to set aside time for yourself and your needs.

This gets a whole lot easier when you realize you can only give what you have. You must take care of yourself so you can take care of your life and your loved ones.

Turn off your phone, shut your door, take time for you, whatever that looks like. **Do it without guilt.**

NO ONE CAN POUR
FROM AN EMPTY CUP.

Every step forward
helps us gain
momentum
against resistance.

BUILD MOMENTUM,
BEGIN

The most important step we can take on the road to living out our **purpose** is to begin. Most people never get past this step. The ability to begin separates, it divides, and it propels.

Beginning requires movement. It requires action. Plans are awesome, but without action, they're just pretty ideas.

Why do we hesitate? Many find it difficult to know where to begin. What's the **first step**? What if we make a mistake? Worse, what if we make a mistake and other people see it?

In my humble opinion, it's not so much what you do with that first step, but the fact that you took it. Being **brave** enough to put yourself out there is something that changes the game.

We gain **momentum** when we begin moving toward our goals. That first step opens the door for more opportunities and more direction along the way. God notices when we allow ourselves to take that first step of faith, however small it may be. The steps that come after get easier as we grow faith in ourselves and our purpose.

Momentum is defined by *Merriam-Webster* as "the impetus of a **moving** object. I confess, I had to look up the definition of impetus. Impetus is "the force by which a body moves against the resistance." I love that!

So when we step out in faith, we are pushing back against a body's natural resistance. Every step forward helps us gain momentum against that resistance.

Determine to take your first step today.

WORDS TO BE BRAVE BY

day 74

YOUR
CHOICES
ARE YOUR
POWER

Qualified

day 75

YOU ARE QUALIFIED

That moment comes when we feel the energy of a new idea, a new dream. It's *exhilarating*. Inside the dream is hope, faith, and excitement. The dream is a seed.

If you're like me, about two minutes after the initial rush, I start disqualifying myself. My mind can dig up everything I've ever done wrong and wave it in my face like a white flag of surrender. It doesn't stop until I'm *convinced* that I am unfit for the purpose at hand. Why do we obsess about not being qualified or capable of doing what we know is right for us?

The root of self-disqualification is fear. It's self-sabotage that begins at the starting gate, crippling us.

What are we afraid of? Failure, for one, but so often, we're more afraid of *success*. Success brings with it a brand-new set of issues. Change, criticism, and increased exposure just to name a few.

Next time you're faced with a chance to *dream* a new dream, don't talk yourself out of it. Instead write a list of why you are perfectly fit for this. Write out your qualifications. Build yourself up in your own mind using your own words.

Walk in the *confidence* of knowing you wouldn't have been given the dream if you weren't qualified to do it.

day 76

FOCUS ON GROWTH RATHER THAN
COMFORT

Take it from me. I'm a pro.

I've spent most of my adult life avoiding discomfort in every way imaginable. If I believed it would make me feel vulnerable, exposed, or open me up to rejection, I would walk, rather, sprint away from the situation. There is a trail of unrealized opportunities following behind me.

My fear of discomfort kept me from stepping out into areas I knew God had **called me** to. I'd spent most of my time trying to stay small and not risk too much.

But I'm here to tell you that avoiding discomfort didn't work. I wound up frustrated and frozen.

I couldn't figure out which **direction** to take. I was frozen because I couldn't see the answers that were staring back at me. I couldn't see them because I would only accept ONE answer, and that was whichever one kept me most comfortable.

Just because something is uncomfortable doesn't mean it isn't right for you.

Comfort has become a **crutch** that allows many of us to opt out of difficult situations, but I think you know you were put on this earth to do hard things.

Being a mother is hard, caring for aging parents is hard, and writing a book is hard. If we stay frozen in the fear of discomfort, we will miss out on so many **beautiful** things that are purposed for our lives.

Society, social media, and the world all have lulled us into thinking the blessed life is the one without struggle, without conflict, and without unmet needs. We've been bamboozled into believing it's easy to get healthy, easy to **succeed**, easy to change the world. That's not true. Life comes with hardships.

Hard things can be **beautiful** and important tools for our progression. The challenges we face have value. It's about who we become on the way to where we're going.

Take a step into those dreams you hold tightly to your heart. **Expect discomfort**. That's how you know you're growing.

BRAVE
FEAR

BRAVE FEAR

Being brave means recognizing fear for what it is: a liar. Fear is a **feeling**. That's it. It's not a premonition of future catastrophe. Being brave means stepping out in faith regardless of your fears and self-doubts.

Fear and trust have a direct link. If you **trust** you are where God wants you to be, what do you have to fear? Sure, you may experience some difficult roads ahead, but difficulty isn't something to be afraid of. You are **capable** of handling life's challenges. Don't let your fear keep you from taking risks and living boldly.

Just because you feel afraid doesn't mean you have a reason for fear. For example, take my completely insane fear of large bridges. I am fairly certain that my automobile will not be blown over the side of a very tall bridge by a gust of wind, but that doesn't quell my anxiety. I'm afraid with very little probability of what I fear actually happening. It's a waste of energy and brain space.

Learn to **move forward** despite your feelings. You weren't created to make decisions based solely on your emotions, especially when you're feeling afraid.

Viewing your future through the lens of fear will keep you immobile. Immobility is the opposite of movement. Movement is **progress**, and we all need more of that in our lives. You can forge ahead bravely and confidently knowing that you were **created** with a purpose, and you have what it takes to walk in it.

day 78

KINDNESS IS THE CURE

Yes, we all have a responsibility to *change* the world. This sounds so daunting. How can anyone affect change on a global scale?

Our current days are filled with all kinds of darkness: natural disasters, poverty, and hate to name a few. This darkness wants to overwhelm the *light* and separate us from each other. So far, it's been doing a pretty good job.

We are responsible for fighting against this darkness with every ounce of our being. We must resist the urge to join in the war of egos so prevalent on every media outlet. What weapon do we use?

Kindness. Kindness is the cure. Kindness is compassion in action. You may think I'm oversimplifying, but hear me out.

Every act of kindness pushes back against the darkness inside of us and inside others. How many people's lives could be *changed* by a simple act of kindness?

Kindness is easy to share. It's free and comes back to you in abundance.

Here's a simple way to begin: starting today, make a *mindful* effort to be kind to people on your daily path, especially the unkind ones. You never know what someone is going through.

You can *change* the world. Be kind.

KINDNESS IS FREE
AND COMES BACK
TO YOU IN
ABUNDANCE.

WHAT DO YOU
truly want?

I've been asking myself this question quite a bit recently. What do I really want in this life? The question is **intimidating**. Some people are too afraid to even ask themselves this. What if we ask and we don't like the answer?

Reflecting on this is a worthwhile exercise because it can reveal whether you are living your authentic life. Most of us will spend a lifetime navigating the path between what we truly want and what we'll settle for.

To know if you're living an **authentic** life, ask yourself these two questions: What do you truly want? What puts the spark in my heart?

Sometimes settling doesn't look like settling to those on the outside. That's okay; they don't need to **understand** it for it to be true for you. Maybe those close to you think you're living a **dream life**, but you know there's still more for you on the path ahead.

Listen to the voice inside calling you to a different, more **fulfilling** place. Make choices and take actions that lead you closer to the life you truly **desire**.

DIMINISH
FEELINGS OF GUILT
BY FORGIVING
YOURSELF.

day 80

GUILT IS A BEAST THAT
KILLS ᴏᴜʀ CONFIDENCE

Time and time again, I come across a woman who struggles regularly with **immense** feelings of guilt. I know because I'm one of them. So often we rehearse mistakes from the past that keep us in the emotional cycle of unnecessary guilt. Chronic guilt keeps us running in circles of self-sabotage, sometimes for years. Unchecked, feeling guilty can become a habit that keeps us shackled in the past.

Don't misunderstand me. Guilt can serve a **healthy** purpose. Guilt is a signal that calls us to examine our behavior and make better choices in the future. In the proper context, guilt can help us grow.

But unnecessary guilt is a confidence-sucking vampire, convincing us that we are **unworthy** of the life and love we truly desire. It's time to stop listening to it. This unwavering guilt sticks around, making sure that we always keep our head down and our dreams untouched. It shutters up our potential and keeps us in hiding. We were not created to hide, not by a long shot.

When those feelings of guilt come up, I try to examine the **source**. What had I been thinking the moment before? What's the narrative going on inside my head? Is the feeling of guilt my soul urging me to set things right, or is it a mind-set of unworthiness trying to keep me down?

Another way to diminish feelings of guilt is to forgive ourselves. We must try to **move past** our mistakes. Hey, we're human; imperfection is in our genetic code. We can't go back in time and change what's happened, so release the regret. There's no room for it where you are going. You don't have control over the past, but you have a great deal of control over your **future**.

day 81

WORRY

If only worry could actually affect the *outcome*, then we might be justified in indulging this joy-stealing beast. But it doesn't. Worry only destroys today, and it does nothing for tomorrow. Its only power is in keeping us distracted and fearful in the present moment, so we aren't living in the now.

I get it. I'm a mom of two young adults. I'm capable of worrying so much that at times it borders on hysteria. I'm a pro at it, always have been. I worry about *big things*, like illness and death, but I can worry over nonsensical things that will likely never happen. Those are my middle of the night worry-session favorites. It takes real obsession to lose a night's sleep worrying about whether or not I mailed an important document. Yes, my anxiety knows no bounds.

The problem is if we allow worry to dominate our thoughts, we will miss out on the wonderful *blessings* already present in our lives. Worry is anxiety, and anxiety doesn't create joy. It can also create unnecessary anxiety for those closest to us. Want to worry my kids? Let them watch their mom go into a worry-induced meltdown.

To combat worry, I try to *focus on the moment* that I'm in. Really sitting in the moment and seeing what is around you can create a fountain of gratitude. We all have something to be thankful for. Maybe that's what worries us the most. There is a joyous beauty to life, to being here on this planet at this very moment. It's not always easy, but wow, what a *splendid* journey it can be.

Being mindful and practicing gratitude is a great antidote to worry. I've found that a positive and negative feeling cannot exist in the same space at the same moment. They can swing back and forth, but they don't ever simultaneously occupy the same space. Dedicate yourself to being *grateful*. Practice it with intention, especially in times of worry.

day 82

PREFER THE COMPANY
of those who prefer you

If you can learn to do this, your life will change. It's **amazing** how much richer and better life can be when you are around people who are truly happy you're alive and value your presence. Yes, they do exist. That's your tribe.

It's easy in this modern life for our relationships to get stuck in a rut. As time goes on and circumstances change, **relationships** change as well. Too often we resist the subtle knowing that this or that person no longer has our best interest at heart, and we're no longer their priority.

As difficult as it may be, there often comes a point in life when we **need** to let go of people who no longer value their relationship with us.

Many of us stay in that dead space for way too long. I know I have.

It's a painful **truth**, but not every relationship you're in now will be with you in the long term. That's okay. Some people weren't meant to stay with you forever, but **thankfully**, some were.

People change and so do their priorities. Let them.

Do yourself a favor and don't stay in a relationship where you're the only one who **wants** to be there. You'll exhaust yourself trying to keep up both sides. It's like trying to play tennis with yourself.

You can't do it . . . not for long anyway.

Let go of those people who leave you feeling bad about yourself and who steal your life's **energy**. They are taking up space that needs to be **available** to new people and experiences. It's okay if your circle is small, probably even better.

Instead, surround yourself with those people who **prefer** you. Seek them out. They're out there looking for you, too.

Open your heart and time to those who want to do life with you.

YOUR
SELF-IMAGE IS
POWERFUL

Day 83

YOUR SELF-IMAGE IS
POWERFUL

I don't hear much about self-image anymore. It seems we've gone from a society that is more concerned with selfie image than our self-image. (I spend a lot of time with teenagers.) Approval is now external, not internal. We are doing ourselves and our children a great disservice.

How we see ourselves is at the core of how we live our lives, the choices we make and the relationships we create. It's how we perceive our own value.

If you don't see yourself as worthy, capable, or good enough, you will not create the life you truly deserve. (Side note, you deserve a fabulous life full of joy, purpose, and love!)

Self-image is always in flux. I think as we go through seasons and changes, it's always good to set aside some time for self-reflection, kind of a checkup on how you see yourself. In my own life, I've had to examine some areas where my self-image wasn't what it should be. Some ideas I carried about myself were so deeply ingrained, I couldn't fathom any other way to be.

It felt like truth, but it wasn't. Truth can handle close inspection; insecurity cannot.

It can be difficult to change those core beliefs about yourself, but you can do it. It takes time, mindfulness, and a little grit. It's your mind, your body, and your life. You get to choose how you see yourself and how you apply that vision to your life.

day 84

don't listen to THE HATERS AND CRITICS. THEY'RE SPEAKING THEIR TRUTH, not yours

Sometimes people will pop into your life and drop their unloving, unsolicited criticism right in your lap. You're left with a heaping pile of self-doubt and fear. Sometimes the criticism comes from people you *love* the most.

Here's something I've learned over the years—don't take it personally. I know it's easier said than done, but it's vital for your success. Their fear and doubt are not yours to *carry*.

These people, some knowingly and some not, are merely looking at you through the lens of their own insecurities and pain. But it's their lens not yours. They haven't risen above their own negative thinking, so they can't *fathom* that you should either. How dare you live your life outside of their pain!

My friend, they are wrong.

Pray for them. Be kind to them. But whatever you do, do not internalize their words. Don't replay them. Don't *consider* them.

Those words don't belong in your head.

Take it from me, this may take a little practice.

One negative comment on social media can have me reeling for days, but the nice words tend to get buried in that mental mud.

Don't let anyone discourage you from the *dreams* and purposes you have in your heart. You have them for a reason, even if others don't understand them.

You don't have to share what's in your heart with everyone. Some people aren't in a place where they can understand you. Give them *grace*, and let it go.

You are the one who gets to tell your story; no one else has that power unless you give it to them.

Listen to your narrative not theirs. Trust your *vision*. It was given to you and not someone else for a reason.

Ouch, That Hurt

OUCH, THAT HURT

Emotional trigger points are *mirrors* into our souls. Listen to them. Observe them. Sit with them awhile. They will tell you a lot about yourself.

We all have been in situations where suddenly something happens that triggers deep, strong *emotions*. If you are like me, you may not even know why you are so upset over something that appears to be so trivial. My guess is you aren't upset about the present circumstances. It's more likely that the present circumstances touched an unhealed wound.

You're a young mom, your toddler throws her plate on the floor, and you have a complete meltdown.

Are you crying because of the mess? Of course not, go deeper.

You're probably crying because you're *exhausted* and unsure of yourself. Maybe you're feeling like you are not cut out for this. Those deeper feelings bubble to the surface, brought to you via your two-year-old.

This kind of situation happens to all of us. A coworker says something or a friend cancels lunch, and there we are, teleported back to second grade feeling obscure, left out, and lonely. Those deeper *feelings* need to be addressed.

Sit with them awhile. *Feel* them. Then let them go.

We all carry wounds from our past. Sometimes we don't even recognize it until we overreact in the present day.

Don't be afraid to go deeper, past those surface-level reactions, to where the hurt originates. That's where the *freedom* is.

YOU ARE NOT AT THE MERCY OF YOUR INADEQUACIES

This was the first original quote I ever shared. I was at a point in my life that I was really struggling with raising teenagers, learning to let go, and preparing for my empty nest. The **feelings** of failure and inadequacy stuck with me like they were branded on my soul.

It felt like everything I said and did was wrong. If I lost my **patience** with my family or missed an important event, those feelings would follow me for days. I was overwhelmed by my own shortcomings and riddled with guilt because of my perceived lack.

It was that moment when I felt God speak to my heart, "You are not at the **mercy** of your inadequacies." Wow, I was struck silent.

You see, we all have shortcomings. We all make mistakes. Some of them are chronic. Those inadequacies are not meant to control you or to **dominate** your thoughts about yourself. I had to learn to quit beating myself up.

You were not created to be **perfect**, and you certainly weren't created to tear yourself down every time you perceived a deficiency in some area of your life.

You are covered in **grace**. You are human. You are only controlled by your inadequacies when you focus on them.

YOU ARE
COVERED IN
grace

WORDS TO BE BRAVE BY

day 87

DON'T LOOK FOR THE PATH OF
LEAST RESISTANCE.
FIND THE PATH
TO YOUR PURPOSE
AND PRESS THROUGH
THE RESISTANCE.

LOVE
IS A VERB

I've said this for years. We can get caught up in the emotion of love when the *action* of love is equally important.

How many of us have let someone we love treat us poorly because of our emotional connection of love? So often we cling to the emotional, the *feelings*, without vetting the behavior of those we love.

I've done it more times than I can count. I'm sure you have, too.

What good is it to share the emotional *connection* of love with someone without the actions that love takes?

Let me explain.

You can share the emotional connection of love, but the person on the other end may not act in a loving way toward you. Some people ignore the need for action all together, *believing* the

feeling should be enough. It may be the case that the other person simply doesn't know how to express love through their actions. Either way, it's no way to live your life and build your relationships.

Love expresses itself through action. Love wants what is best for you. Love is a verb. It isn't stagnant; it moves and grows.

True love isn't just about feelings. True love doesn't accept neglect or abuse in a relationship. Love and neglect cannot coexist in the same space.

The highest of all is the action of love. What good is it to feel love toward someone who doesn't act lovingly back?

Love isn't always affectionate, and oftentimes it will challenge you and tell you hard truths. But most of all, love is a catalyst of growth.

Focus on
SOLUTIONS
AND YOU WILL FIND
SOLUTIONS.

YOU ATTRACT
WHAT YOU FOCUS ON

I truly believe that we are walking, talking, giant **magnets**. We attract to us what we spend our time focusing on. Want more problems? Spend your **time** hyper-focused on your problems, and that is what you will get. Unfortunately, I've tried the "hyper-focus, freak out over my issues" approach only to see that I've made the situation an even bigger mess.

Make a conscious choice today to shift your **focus**. Where is your attention going?

What we focus on we are **training** our minds to see. I don't know about you, but I want to see the good, the positive, and the lovely.

Focus on the parts of your life that are good. Focus on what you want more of in your life. Instead of honing in on your dress size, why not hone in on your warm smile and your ability to make friends easily. Instead of concentrating on a negative issue at work, try **looking** for ways to improve. Be solution oriented not problem oriented.

Focusing on your problems leads to nothing but frustration (and possibly a late-night binge on mint chocolate chip ice cream). Trust me, neither of those will bring you the life you desire.

Focus on **solutions** and you will find solutions. Focus on the positive and you will find more to be positive about.

What are some areas in your life where you need to **shift** your focus?

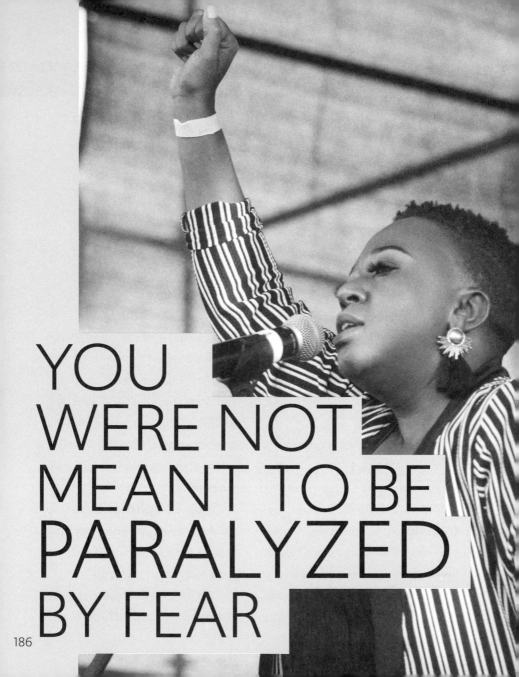

YOU
WERE NOT
MEANT TO BE
PARALYZED
BY FEAR

YOU WERE NOT MEANT TO BE
PARALYZED BY FEAR

Every single one of us is familiar with fear. It's part of the human condition.

None of our fears is original to us. We fear many of the same things. Fear of failure—check, fear of the unknown—check, and my all-time favorite, fear of change.

The goal is not to let your fears **control** you. What if we all accomplished what was in our hearts despite fear? **Imagine** the type of world we would live in.

Step out into those things you know you're meant for. Don't let fear paralyze your life and hold you back from walking in the fullness of your **purpose**.

The world is waiting on brave ones like you to step forward and bring about true and **lasting** change. We all feel the fear, but don't let it stop you. Instead, **focus** on the truth.

You were created with a purpose, **designed** to impact the world for good.

Trust Yourself

TRUST YOURSELF

To get anywhere in this life, you need to believe in yourself. We hear this all the time, but that's because it's true. Without the *fundamental* trust in your ability to accomplish your dreams, you will be constantly stuck and waiting on your dreams to be served up without any action on your part.

Nobody can *believe* for you. They can support you, they can pray for you, but their belief can't replace your own. What's between your mind and your heart is what matters most. What do you believe about yourself?

Trust your ideas. Trust your abilities. This is especially true when those ideas aren't perfect or predictable. Trusting yourself means believing you can handle uncertainty and setbacks just as easily as you can handle the big *victories* in life.

Step out in faith, believing that every experience is helping you get you where you want to go. It's especially important with the plans that didn't work. There is a lot of *valuable* information hidden inside failure. Failure is a moment of learning and not a valid reason to stop trusting yourself.

You are capable of living the dreams you imagine when lying awake at night. You will need to learn and grow along the way, but the *dreams* are yours to fulfill.

You must believe that the ideas you feel in your heart are the truth of who you are. Then you must act on that belief. Those beliefs are the backbone of your decisions. Your decisions direct your actions. Your actions create your life.

Trust yourself. Trust God and the path he has for you. Put yourself out there. You will do some things wrong, but you will also do some things right. Learn, *let go*, and keep believing.

CHOOSE *to look*
FOR THE POSITIVE
in every MOMENT.

THE POSITIVE SIDE TO STAYING POSITIVE

Positive thinking is powerful. It doesn't mean refusing to see the negative or living in a wonderland where you're free to live a life without hard situations. A good attitude doesn't get you a "get out of jail free" card, but it can set you free from the prison of mental negativity and overthinking.

Positive thinking is so much more than that. It's a way of managing one's attitudes and emotions. Staying positive in the midst of turmoil isn't delusional; it's life-altering.

Positive thinking opens the door to **opportunity** and change. By having a positive attitude, you stay open to the best possible outcomes in a negative situation. A positive outlook says: Yes, times are tough right now, but I have hope. I have hope in the goodness that is yet to come, so please send me some **goodness** straightaway.

A negative mind-set holds you prisoner inside of your own head, draining your energy and your insight all at once. It's not so easy to see solutions to your problems, or even a more productive way of dealing with the situation, when your mind is trapped in a loop of negativity.

Develop a positive attitude by **training** yourself to look for the good in every situation. You may be in a situation that is anything but good. We all have something to be thankful for, something to appreciate. Focus on that. **Choose** to look for the positive in every moment.

SET YOURSELF UP FOR SUCCESS

You have goals you want to reach one day; we all do. Success in any area usually requires millions of **small steps** and small victories that will lead to your higher goals. Rarely have I seen one or two giant steps lead to immediate achievement. If that's you, you have my undying admiration.

All the work required to meet your goals is going to take a lot of mental and physical **energy**. Successful accomplishments usually require more of us than we initially expected to give. That's why it's so important to give yourself a good foundation for achieving your goals.

It starts with the **basics**.

Take care of your body. I can't stress this enough. If you don't feel good, nothing else works. How you **feel** regulates the energy you put into your day, and thus, your life. Most of us need better habits when it comes to self-care. I know I do.

Get enough sleep, drink water, and please get a little movement in your day. Your body will thank you and you'll be more **productive**. The hydration struggle is real, my friend.

Spend more time doing those activities that make you feel like a **winner**. Invest in your own self-confidence. Do more of what makes you feel grateful to be alive.

Be enthusiastic and get **excited** about your life. Show up with every ounce of energy you've got. There's no room for halfway when you want something. If you want to go to the top in any area of your life, you must go **all in.**

DO WHAT MAKES
YOU FEEL

grateful

TO BE ALIVE.

day 94

YOU CAN'T BE
everything
TO EVERYONE

What would happen if instead of making everyone around us happy, we focused on our own *happiness*?

Many of us live with a false sense of obligation that we must *meet* every need that exists in our circle of relationships. I dare call it an epidemic. We place everyone else's happiness and care above our own.

I've lived this, and I can tell you, it's exhausting. No person on this earth is meant to spend their life's *energy* running around making sure everyone else gets what they need while ignoring their own needs and happiness.

It isn't selfish to focus on your happiness. Nobody likes that. I'm talking about taking responsibility for your own *joy* and letting

those around you do the same. The odds are that you are probably doing so much for so many people, that they too think you need to give yourself some of your own attention. This is for you, wives, mothers, and caregivers. I know we want to be *everything* to everyone we love, but we can't. They have their own journeys to joy, as do we.

Truthfully, you can never make anyone else happier than they choose to be. So why not find the joy in your life and *build* a tent there?

day 95

HOW DO YOU
PERCEIVE THE WORLD
AROUND YOU?

Perception is everything. The way we perceive the world and our place in it is the *foundation* of our beliefs. Our beliefs construct our attitudes. Our attitudes are what determine our choices. Our choices determine our lives.

The way we perceive the world guides our *decisions* about what opportunities to accept, doors to walk through, and even how we take care of our bodies.

How do you view the world?

Do you view it as a generally bad place full of potential pain and fear? Or do you see the world as a beautiful, albeit imperfect, place *filled* with opportunities for growth and goodness?

For many of us, our perception could use a little filtering. We blow up and hyper-focus on the negativity around us and completely glance over the awesome *beauty* found in everyday life. Our perception of the world directly correlates with how we perceive ourselves.

It's difficult to envision the world *full* of mostly pain and scarcity, then to turn around and view the opposite for ourselves.

How we view the world, our perception, will have a huge impact on the quality of our lives. It comes down to choosing what we *hold* in our minds. Surely there are terrible things happening in the world around us, but simultaneously there are good things. There is war, but there is also childbirth. There is fear, but also *friendship*. We don't have to ignore the ugly parts, rather, let the lovely and the good take up more space in our minds.

Do you need to change the lens through which you view the world?

KEEP SHOWING UP FOR YOURSELF

KEEP SHOWING UP FOR YOURSELF

Want to see **lasting change** in an area of your life? You will need to make a commitment to the most important person in your life. That would be you, in case you've forgotten.

I can't say this enough…to myself. You must **commit** to keep showing up for yourself, even on the hard days. Especially on the hard days. Half of being successful in life is just showing up again and again. It is about picking yourself up and pressing forward to the next mark. Life is a series of getting knocked down and getting back up.

Trying to get healthy? **Commit** to it, even when you've had a setback. Want to write a book? Commit to working on it daily.

Commit to yourself by taking actions toward **achieving** your goals. Hold yourself to that commitment even when you don't feel like it. Set your mind to do what needs to be done, no matter what.

Many women quit on themselves right before the realization of their dreams. Don't let that be you. Commitment to yourself is the **determination** that you will not quit, even in challenging times. That's how you'll create **lasting** change in your life.

Expectations

day 97

EXPECTATIONS

I hope you walk through your life with **hopeful** expectancy. I hope you expect goodness from every situation and every person you meet. Expectations are a good thing. They **motivate** us and give our hope a vision. Expectations work side by side with our intentions.

While en route to your dreams, it's important to manage your **expectations**. I don't mean that you lower your ambitions to be more reasonable. Reasonable is overrated. However, try not to get overly invested in one single activity. Don't let one small letdown derail your entire **goal**.

Expect big things. Expect your goals to be met, but also realize that there will be times you'll be let down. It's **inevitable**. That doesn't mean you should quit.

Expectations can be tricky. It's a balance between belief in your goals and understanding the process is **unpredictable**. To be clear, I'm not talking about expectations in your relationships. That's a matter better explained by a more qualified person. It's about managing your expectations when being let down after you did your best; you had **faith**, and things still didn't work out the way you hoped. When you encounter an unrealized expectation, pull yourself up and keep expecting **good things** to come your way.

day 98

SOMETIMES WE NEED A
Little UNDOING

Life has a way of nudging us *forward*, even when we are quite comfortable where we are. I've played many roles in life, but "author" isn't one of them. When opportunity knocked, I opened the door and here we are.

At that moment, I became a little undone because I was going *outside* of my comfort zone.

During the writing process, I began to remember long forgotten moments of my childhood when I wrote poetry and short stories. I hadn't thought about writing in decades. I was so removed that I barely recognized that part of myself.

Those ideas were buried under years of *neglect* and fear.

Don't keep your gifts hidden away from the world. What's inside you is too important. Peel back the layers of self-doubt and fear. Get a little *undone*. Get a little uncomfortable.

What hidden treasures have you buried? What *special* gift have you neglected?

Have you pushed down the *potential* that exists inside of you? Dig deep and unearth the talents and gifts you've buried. Bring them out and show the world what you can do.

DON'T KEEP YOUR
GIFTS
HIDDEN AWAY FROM
THE WORLD.

Learn from
those who have
generously shared
their knowledge
with the world.

day 99

KEEP LEARNING

It's vital to your **success** to commit yourself to increasing your knowledge. No one has all the information they need to live up to their full potential. That means you need to be actively **looking** for ways to learn as much as you can about the topics that will help along the way.

Devote time to reading and studying information that relates to your goals. Trying to lose weight? Read nutritional books. Want to make more money? Listen to podcasts of successful people. Thanks to the internet, we're information rich. I often criticize the influence of the internet on modern life, but when it comes to sharing important knowledge, it has **enhanced** our society. Take advantage of the technology available to help you expand your thinking. If you don't have the time for reading, try audio books during your daily commute. It's a great way to be exposed to new ideas while not adding extra hours to your day.

Learn from those who have **generously** shared their knowledge with the world. Glean their wisdom to help you along on the road to **achieving** your goals.

day100

YOUR STORY MATTERS

Your story is the *narrative* of your journey and time here on earth. Every person on this planet has a point of view and a story to tell. Everyone has something *meaningful* to share. That includes you!

What you have overcome and the way you did it can *inspire* or encourage someone else going through difficulties. You never know which detail, however small to you, can help another person.

All our lives are *connected*, and we need each other. Your story isn't just about you. It's about all the people you will touch while on your path.

Tell your story. Express it in whatever way feels *natural* to you. Let it out. You don't have to be a writer or have a platform to communicate your story to others. If you are an artist, paint. If you are a gardener, grow. What you're passionate about is an expression of you and your *journey*.

Don't be afraid to share. Our stories are connected and remind us that we're not journeying alone. Don't be afraid to be *brave*. You were made for this.

MY
BE BRAVE
LIST

_____

_____

_____

_____

_____

_____

SPREAD BRAVERY

If you've been inspired by the lessons of bravery in this book, please share them on social media.

- Don't waste another precious minute of your life rejecting yourself #GirlBeBrave #WordsToBeBraveBy

- The person you have the closest, most intimate relationship with is yourself #GirlBeBrave #WordsToBeBraveBy

- There is no "someday" when it comes to action #GirlBeBrave #WordsToBeBraveBy

- Momentum joins us when we take action #GirlBeBrave #WordsToBeBraveBy

- This is your reminder that it's okay to say no. #GirlBeBrave #WordsToBeBraveBy

- Dream chasing is not for the halfhearted #GirlBeBrave #WordsToBeBraveBy

- Grit is committed determination. #GirlBeBrave #WordsToBeBraveBy

- Nothing good comes from diminishing yourself. EVER. #GirlBeBrave #WordsToBeBraveBy

- Move yourself in the direction of your dreams #GirlBeBrave #WordsToBeBraveBy

- You don't have to be bulletproof to take a leap of faith. You need only to be brave #GirlBeBrave #WordsToBeBraveBy

- Kindness is free and comes back to you in abundance #GirlBeBrave #WordsToBeBraveBy

- Focus on solutions and you will find solutions #GirlBeBrave #WordsToBeBraveBy

- Do what makes you feel grateful to be alive #GirlBeBrave #WordsToBeBraveBy

- Don't keep your gifts hidden away from the world #GirlBeBrave #WordsToBeBraveBy

- Learn from those who have generously shared their knowledge with the world #GirlBeBrave #WordsToBeBraveBy

ACKNOWLEDGEMENTS

The opportunity to write this book was quite a pleasant surprise. I truly believe it was an opportunity presented to me by God, and with that belief, I knew I had to proceed forward with it.

There were so many instrumental people along the way that made it possible for me to go on this journey. I'd like to thank Karen Longino, and the Abingdon Press team for their belief in the message of Girl Be Brave. You saw it even when I did not. I'd also like to thank my editor Natalie for her patient guidance through the writing process.

I'd like to acknowledge my husband Jeff, his constant support and belief in me during our marriage. I am forever grateful for his trust in me. I also want to acknowledge my children Hunter and Madison. You have both taught me so much. On the days that I feel as though I can't do anything right, your faces remind me to keep going.

I wouldn't be here without the example set by the women in my family: grandmothers, aunts, cousins and all of the other women who have set a positive example for me. My grandmother Frances and my mother both showed me how to live in strength facing adversity. You taught me how to overcome. Thank you.

I'd also like to thank my shop ladies Amy, Jill, Julie, Savanah, and Wende. You helped me make it through some very tough times through your commitment to keep things going while I took the time to write this book.

I appreciate every single one of you, and I know God brought you into my life for such a time as this.

ABOUT THE AUTHOR

Cheryl Hale is a writer, artist, designer, businesswoman, and mom. Southern born and raised; she loves big hats and southern cooking. Hale was inspired to launch her blog and online store after coming across her grandmother Frances' Bible, with a letter written in the back that said *girl be brave*. Passionate about impacting the lives of women everywhere, she has established a Girl Be Brave scholarship in her grandmother's honor, funded by profits from her product line. Cheryl now lives in Mobile, Alabama with her husband and two kids, where she chases four dogs and a cat around her garden and continues to share her story on **https://girlbebrave.com/blog/**. *Girl Be Brave* is her first book.

PHOTO CREDITS

#girlbebrave